Patients Matter Most and Dr. Rosenberg

both an essential introduction and an enduring reference to the subject for the entire healthcare community, extending from policymakers, administrators, practitioners, trainees, ethicists, and indeed, patients."

—RODERICK MCINNES, OC, MD, PHD, FRSC

Alva Chair in Human Genetics, McGill University

Past President, American Society of Human Genetics

Past Acting President, Canadian Institutes of Health Research

"Dr. Lawrence Rosenberg is one of healthcare's visionary thinkers, grounded in the quality care of patients as a renowned surgeon and trialed by fire, leading complex health organizations. In *Patients Matter Most*, he lays out clearly how technology and digitization are fundamentally altering the healthcare industry. He shares how this will continue to evolve a more empowered patient and promote a realignment of the many elements of healthcare and, increasingly, the health *and* social care *network*. He predicts a continuing disintermediation, bringing health and health-impacting social services more directly to the patient, eliminating the "middleman," the associated cost, and bureaucracy. This will threaten the status quo for many nodes in the health and social services network, but Dr. Rosenberg's clear-eyed and experience-informed perspectives offer an important set of considerations for health leaders and policymakers as they address what is becoming an unsustainable industry."

—JAMES B. PEAKE, MD

Lieutenant General, USA (Ret.)

40th US Army Surgeon General

6th US Secretary of Veterans Affairs

"Dr. Lawrence Rosenberg draws from his storied career as a medical scientist, transplant surgeon, and leading medical-system innovator to intertwine his personal story with a brilliant, yet lucid analysis of the complexity faced by healthcare systems across the globe. Everyone understands at some level that solutions to these challenges must focus on serving the individual and not budgets, guidelines, and averages. Good ideas abound, but tractable approaches are needed. From the crucible of his caring for one patient at a time to serving the vast medical and social needs of a major metropolitan area, Dr. Rosenberg offers specific insights and prescriptions for making disease and wellness care personal, efficient, and effective. Anyone, anywhere on the planet who is interested in improving healthcare should read this book."

—ALEXANDER FLEMING, MD
Founder and Executive Chairman, Kinexum
Founder and CEO, Kitalys Institute
Former Head of the US Food and Drug Administration's
Endocrinology and Metabolic Division

"This new book on healthcare from Dr. Lawrence Rosenberg brings a fresh picture to the evolving world of healthcare. As the head of several organizations, he has been following and leading the evolving changes in healthcare. He carefully notes the evolution of technology and healthcare, and he illustrates the importance of evolving networks within joint hospital systems. Most importantly, this volume works to demonstrate how medical knowledge can promote competition between nurses, family docs, and specialist physicians working with the best examples in Canada, the US, and Europe. It demonstrates a wide range of medical knowledge and promotes competition for the best patient outcomes within evolving network methodologies."

—TERRENCE SULLIVAN, PHD
Doctor of Science, Honoris Causa
Former Chair of the Board, Canadian Agency for Drugs and Technologies in Health
Former President and CEO, Cancer Care Ontario

"As an advocate for best-in-class patient care and peer support for over 70 years, I am awed by the advances in technology that enable healthcare workers and patients to share medical information and connect remotely not just across hospital sites, but across time zones. With proper safeguards in place, technology is undeniably beneficial, empowering patients to have more control of their health and potentially leading to better outcomes. Anything that puts patients in charge of their health deserves our full support."

—SHEILA KUSSNER, OC, OQ, COM
Founder, Hope & Cope

Patients Matter Most

Patients Matter Most

HOW HEALTHCARE IS BECOMING PERSONAL AGAIN

DR. LAWRENCE ROSENBERG

Forbes | Books

Published by Forbes Books, Charleston, South Carolina.
Member of Advantage Media.

Forbes Books is a registered trademark, and the Forbes Books colophon is a trademark of Forbes Media, LLC.

Printed in the United States of America.

10 9 8 7 6 5 4 3 2 1

ISBN: 978-1-95588-417-4 (Hardcover)
ISBN: 979-8-88750-003-4 (eBook)

LCCN: 2023900085

Cover design by Hampton Lamoureux.
Layout design by Matthew Morse.

This custom publication is intended to provide accurate information and the opinions of the author in regard to the subject matter covered. It is sold with the understanding that the publisher, Forbes Books, is not engaged in rendering legal, financial, or professional services of any kind. If legal advice or other expert assistance is required, the reader is advised to seek the services of a competent professional.

Since 1917, Forbes has remained steadfast in its mission to serve as the defining voice of entrepreneurial capitalism. Forbes Books, launched in 2016 through a partnership with Advantage Media, furthers that aim by helping business and thought leaders bring their stories, passion, and knowledge to the forefront in custom books. Opinions expressed by Forbes Books authors are their own. To be considered for publication, please visit **books.Forbes.com**.

Hospitals are only an intermediate stage of civilization, never intended ... to take in the whole sick population. May we hope that the day will come ... when every poor sick person will have the opportunity of a share in a district sick-nurse at home.

—FLORENCE NIGHTINGALE

*To my patients, and especially to those closest to me,
from whom I learned how to practice medicine
and the meaning of life.*

Contents

Acknowledgments 1

Foreword 5

Introduction. 11

CHAPTER 1

Healthcare Reborn: A Predictable, Unstoppable Disruption . . . 15

CHAPTER 2

Understanding the Complexity of Systems and Networks 27

CHAPTER 3

Digitalization and Real-Time Health Systems. 41

CHAPTER 4

Precision Medicine: Why It's Personal Now 55

CHAPTER 5

Decentralization Is Driving Changing Circumstances 67

CHAPTER 6

Democratization of Knowledge 81

CHAPTER 7

Democratization of Technology 93

CHAPTER 8

The Devolution of Control. 107

CHAPTER 9

Moving toward Sustainability. 121

CHAPTER 10

Virtual Care—Not In-Person but Still Personal 139

CHAPTER 11

The Issue of Privacy and Autonomy 153

CHAPTER 12

What Now? 165

Conclusion. 175
About the Author. 179

Acknowledgments

Writing about healthcare for the general public, policymakers, educators, and students has been an exceptional challenge. Given the nature of my practice, the long hours, erratic schedule, and unanticipated but inevitable complications, I somehow never managed to take a step back to reflect on what contribution I was making to the greater good. That is, what was I actually doing to make the system better? For that matter, the system in which I practiced seemed increasingly to be a moving target with no one in control and no one accountable, as if it had taken on a life of its own. And that is when it hit me. I had spent a few years learning about complexity science, and the evolving nature of healthcare seemed to describe the emergence of a complex, adaptive system. This certainly got my attention, and these nascent birth pangs led to the idea for this book.

Creating this book has been a wondrous journey, not only for the clarity it provided, but for self-discovery, as well. I have spent years writing grant applications, scientific articles, and book chapters, but this was my first experience producing a complete book.

The process in which I became immersed reminded me of the story the Talmud tells of Rabbi Yehoshua ben Hanania who asked a young man sitting at a crossroad, "Which is the way to the town?"

The young man pointed to one of the paths and said, "This way is short, but long. The other is long, but short." Yehoshua ben Hanania set out on the first path, quickly arrived at the town, but found his way blocked by gardens and orchards. He then returned to the young man and said, "Didn't you tell me that this path was short?" "I did," said the young man, "but I also warned you that it was long." Fortunately, I've been helped by some very astute and patient people with the experience to guide me, so to speak, to take the long road that eventually gets you to your destination rather than the short one that doesn't, even though it looks as if it does!

Thank you to DeVasha Lloyd, the vice president of membership development at Forbes Books, who reached out to me repeatedly over several months before I would agree to consider writing a book. When she finally pinned me down, I described for her how healthcare was experiencing a once-in-a-generation disintermediation. She was both bewildered and enthralled. It was a word she had never heard before. But once I explained, she was sure there was a book to be written. So, here it is. Thank you, DeVasha, for your persistence.

Associate managing editor Laura Rashley was a pleasure to work with. What a refreshing combination of energy, attention to detail, and sheer joy. Thank you for being there to field all my questions and for keeping our train on the tracks.

I was extremely fortunate to work with Howard Goldberg, my writing partner. Howard, your laid-back style together with a shrewd and penetrating wit really helped to bring this book to life. I learned much from your probing style and insightful comments.

I am grateful to my colleague, Thomas Schlich, currently Chair of the Department of Social Studies of Medicine at McGill University. A fortuitous introduction several years ago gave rise to very rich intellectual collaborations that included an international workshop entitled "Medicine without Doctors: Disintermediation and Patient Agency," which no doubt crystallized my thinking and lit the fuse that led to this book.

Thank you to Francine Dupuis, who worked by my side to build our healthcare and social services network over the past seven years. You are the consummate clinical-operations magician. Many of the ideas expressed in this book were thoroughly dissected through our numerous early morning meetings and late-night text messaging. You taught me more than you know.

Eric Maldoff, thank you for years of rigorous discussion and debate about health systems, politics, and the vicissitudes of life. You gave freely of your valuable time, and our interactions were as close to Socratic learning or formal Talmudic exegesis that I could ever have hoped to experience. The rigor and logic of this book is perhaps proof that I was listening.

To my mother, thank you for giving me a love of books that has remained with me throughout my life and for continuing to be my biggest booster. Perhaps beginning to speak at the age of five was not a constraint after all.

Finally, thank you to my wife, Donna, for all your love and support. Your incredible enthusiasm for reading (and rereading) each and every draft of the text was simply amazing to observe, and the pure joy you derived was awe inspiring. Of course, I always suspected that your unstated design was to have the final say about any copy you were shown. Mission accomplished, my dear.

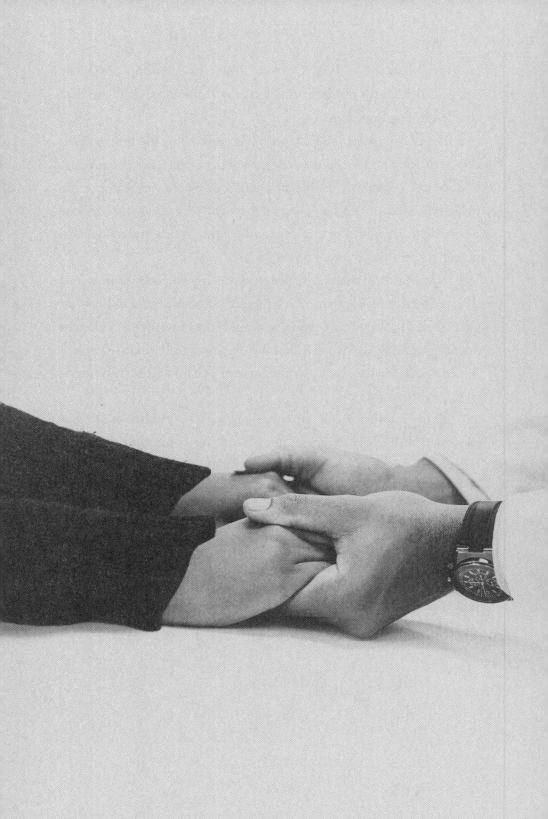

Foreword

There is a long tradition in Western medicine in which patients matter most. For a long time, patients took a leading role in the medical encounter. In the 1700s, patients were the "patrons" of their doctors, paying them an annual fee to be looked after. In this setting, the doctor was economically dependent on his patients. Consultations took place in the patient's home. The patients set the agenda. The doctor interpreted and understood the disease based on the patient's personal experience. Symptoms like pain, swollen ankles, or weight loss determined the diagnosis. Tuberculosis, for example, was called "consumption," describing the protracted decline the patient was going through. Such a diagnosis was highly individualized. It was about the individual patient's disease, taking into account their predisposition, their way of life, their specific environment, and their behavior.

Therapy and prevention were equally individualized. Many therapeutic measures aimed at rebalancing the juices of the patient's body, the humors. This could happen through diet or through a change of one's way of life. It could also be achieved by bloodletting, which was applied to remediate an excess of a particular humor or evacuate "corrupted" humors. The patient's individuality was absolutely central for an effective treatment of his or her ailment. Moreover, patients were actively involved in setting up their treatment plan. They often knew a lot about medicine as part of their general education. Doctors and patients shared the same language about the body and its diseases. The idea of "rebalancing" the humors is an example of this common language. This kind of doctor-patient relationship was not universal, though. University-educated doctors were rare. They were expensive and only accessible to patients of a certain wealth and social standing. Most of the population consulted other healthcare providers out of a wide spectrum of practitioners that included barber-surgeons, apothecaries, drug peddlers, bonesetters, midwives, clerics, and all kinds of people with some expertise or training.

The situation was very different in the hospitals of the early 19th century, especially those in postrevolution Paris. Originally all-purpose welfare institutions, hospitals had become more and more medical over time. By around 1800, the majority of hospitals' inmates were in need of medical care. At that time, doctors had started to discover hospitals as places for training and research. Since hospitals were still primarily charitable institutions, their patients there were indigent. They went to a hospital because they had no other place to go. This meant that they were not in a position to negotiate the rules of how they were treated. Doctors had access to their bodies for examination while they were alive and for dissection after their death. A contemporary characterized this as the "tacit contract" that patients underwrote when they entered the institution.

Within this setting, a new approach to understanding disease emerged. Disease was no longer based on the patients' symptoms. It was now seen as change—a lesion—of an organ or of tissue inside of the patient's body. Historians call this a "localist" approach because the disease was now located at a specific place in the body. Tuberculosis was redefined after the little tubers, *tubercles*, that doctors would find in their organs when they dissected the patients after their death. If tubercles were present, then the condition was tuberculosis. If not, it was some other disease. But how could doctors know about this while the patient was still alive? For this purpose, they developed the methods of physical examination, embodied by the classic four techniques that are still being taught to all medical students: inspection—looking, palpation—feeling, percussion—tapping, and auscultation—listening. All these procedures aimed at identifying the lesion in the interior of the patient's body. This would yield the diagnosis. In cases of tuberculosis, it was mostly auscultation that helped doctors discover the ravages that this affliction wreaked in the lungs of its victims.

This "clinical-pathological" approach to defining disease by organ lesions was first developed in the hospitals of Paris but quickly came to dominate all fields of medicine in the western world. It replaced the older classification according to the symptoms experienced by the patients. The new view went along with a thorough deindividualization of disease. Patients no longer had their own individual disease. They had the same tuberculosis as any other patient. They became a "case" of this disease. This was enabled by the social conditions in the Paris hospitals where the patient was the doctor's social inferior and autopsies, as well as physical examinations, became the routine.

Here is where technology came in. For one of the procedures of physical examination, a technical object became crucial. For auscultation, René Laennec invented the stethoscope in 1916 in Paris. Laennec's stethoscope was just a simple piece of wood with a bell-shaped opening on one end, and it's still being used in this form by modern midwives. The binaural stethoscope that we know today was introduced later. This simple object enabled Laennec to listen to the sounds of the lungs and the heart without too much inconvenience. It helped him to determine what was going on inside his patients' bodies while they were alive. The stethoscope thus reflected the new localist understanding of disease. But the stethoscope also unfolded its own dynamic. It rearranged the choreography of the medical encounter. Using the stethoscope condemned the patients to a passive, subordinate role. They had to follow the instructions of the doctor, who would ask them to breathe, to stop breathing, or to cough. The patients themselves had no access to the information that the doctor was retrieving with the stethoscope. Only the doctor would hear the sound.

In any case, with the new understanding of disease, the patient wouldn't have known how to interpret that information. The new disease concept was full of language that only a medically trained person would understand. No more shared knowledge between doctor and patient. Auscultation reflected the new type of patient-doctor relationship, but it also contributed to it.

Of course, the stethoscope was not the last piece of technology that was integrated into the medical encounter, nor was it the last such technology to deepen the divide between patient and doctor. What comes to mind is the X-ray, discovered in 1895 and immediately applied to medicine. Other examples are blood-pressure measurement, electrocardiograms, electroencephalograms, and many more. Laboratory tests in particular added a whole new category of tools to the medical armamentarium. At the same time, the laboratory was also a new place for creating authoritative knowledge in medicine.

In his laboratory, Robert Koch in 1882 discovered the bacterium that was the cause of tuberculosis. Now tuberculosis was no longer defined by the presence of tubercles. The disease was defined by its cause, the tubercle bacillus. The ultimate diagnostic proof that a given patient's disease was indeed tuberculosis was taken out of the hands of the ordinary doctor. It now came from the laboratory. Over a period of about 200 years, the growth of technology in medicine thus translated into a loss of autonomy and power for the patient. The knowledge gap between doctor and patient widened. Diagnosis lost its individual character and became increasingly standardized.

However, surprisingly, the trend has been reversed in the past 20 years, as we can learn from Dr. Rosenberg's book. Patients have gained in power and autonomy exactly by adopting new technologies. Through newly emerging technology, patients have gained access to medical knowledge. They can monitor their body functions and their health directly. They can even treat themselves. In many situations, the doctor is absent now, cut out of the medical encounter, in the same way that the taxi central is cut out of the relationship between driver and client, the bookstore between publisher and reader, or the journalist between the source of information and its use. Such developments come with opportunities but also with risks, as these nonmedical examples show.

We need guidance and advice in this new world of medicine, and who can be better positioned than the author of this book, who has been in the thick of it for decades; someone who has seen it develop and who is one of the people who has been in charge of the decisions about when and how to apply new technology. Dr. Rosenberg's book is a passionate and thoughtful appeal to take on the challenges of the new world of healthcare, to ride the new wave of technology rather than being submerged by it and turn it into an opportunity to make patients matter most (again).

—THOMAS SCHLICH

Chair, Department of Social Studies of Medicine, McGill University

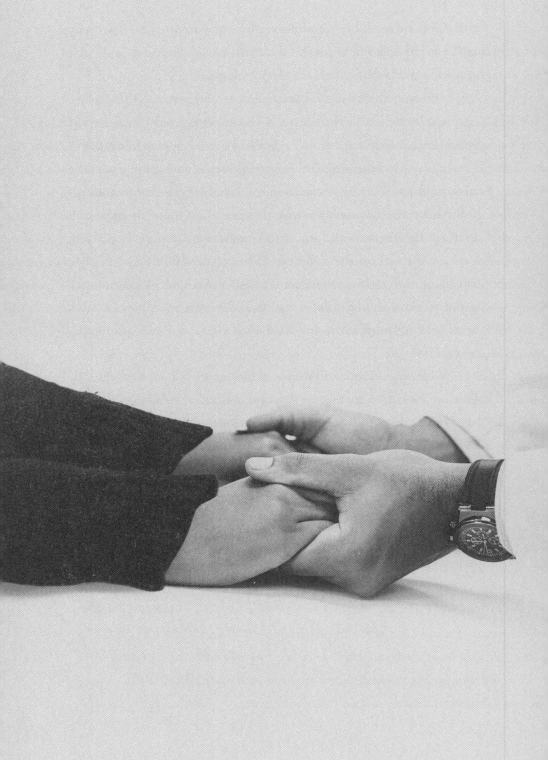

Introduction

After I finished medical school in Montreal and completed a six-year general surgical residency there, I had more than a month to kill in 1985 before I would start training for two years in Michigan as a transplant surgeon. To put food on the table, because I was no longer earning anything, I accepted a temporary job where I would be the only general surgeon in Canada's eastern Arctic. Being in a small community hospital with one operating room was quite a change from working in downtown Montreal's world-class cluster of research and teaching hospitals. I was somewhat apprehensive about the challenge that would be presented by three types of emergencies in the Arctic, and sure enough, I encountered all three.

The last day I was there, I had to do my first cesarean section. The procedure was very different from surgeries I was accustomed to because opening a full-term uterus causes blood and fluid to fly all over the place, and the surgeon's priority is not to stop the bleeding but to focus on the baby and the umbilical cord. My discomfort must have been obvious to those assisting, as word spread afterward that "mother, baby, and surgeon are doing fine." I also was worried about not being equipped to deal with a vascular injury. Someone who came in with a dislocated knee fracture had an obstructed artery, and while

I could relocate the knee, we urgently had to fly the patient down to Montreal for vascular surgery, which did not happen soon enough. My third fear was treating a head injury, but that ended up with a fantastically positive outcome.

An 11-year-old girl had fallen off the back of a three-wheel all-terrain vehicle and was brought in comatose and barely breathing. Our choice was to let her die or open her head and try to deal with what was going on. But this wasn't a *real* hospital, and I was a general surgeon, not a neurosurgeon. The last time I'd seen the inside of somebody's head was in the anatomy lab in first-year medical school 10 years earlier. I took her to the operating room, and an anesthesiologist who was also doing a temporary stint at the hospital put her to sleep. I did what I knew by rote to do, opening up part of her cranium, identifying a bleeding artery, and tying it off. The next day we created a makeshift intensive care unit for her in the back of a commercial airliner. A pediatric resident from Montreal was there with me, and he flew back with her to Montreal with the girl on a respirator. I heard nothing for about 12 weeks, by which time I was in Ann Arbor engaged in my transplant fellowship. Then one day I got a phone call telling me that the girl had walked out of the Montreal Children's Hospital as if nothing had ever happened to her.

We associate the miracles of modern medicine with hospitals, especially the leading university hospitals where I spent the rest of

> The purpose of this book is to help readers connect the dots between parallel developments in technology and in healthcare delivery. These connections bring inevitable changes affecting all of us, everywhere in the world.

my career once I got out of the eastern Arctic. I could regale you with triumphant stories from the operating room, but I have a more urgent message to get out in this book, and it involves healthcare more likely to take place in your living room or over a videocall as in a hospital. The purpose of this book is to help readers connect the dots between parallel developments in technology and in healthcare delivery. These connections bring inevitable changes affecting all of us, everywhere in the world. I expect readers will find this book enlightening regardless of whether they work in healthcare delivery or policymaking. Anyone who goes to a doctor, clinic, or hospital or is wondering about new self-diagnostic technology, virtual visits, and other online tools will learn how and why disruptive changes in healthcare are happening.

It used to be that certain technology resided only in large medical centers and could be used only by certain people. You'll learn all about why that's no longer true. Similarly, medical knowledge that used to reside in the minds of medical specialists has been democratized and often is available to less credentialed providers or even to anyone skilled at searching intelligently for it online. I'll put these developments into historical perspective in chapter 1 to show why they are happening outside our control in somewhat predictable ways.

Healthcare delivery has long been described as a system, which can imply that institutions and individuals have preordained, set roles, but this book calls for reimagining those roles. The system is evolving, and people who understand what is happening are better positioned to take advantage of the changes. The opportunity for individuals to take ownership of their healthcare is unprecedented. For those of us who deliver healthcare or administer various aspects of the system, the message will be that it's time to reset our expectations for what we can control. Doctors will no longer have the near monopoly on medical knowledge that imbued the profession when I earned my MD in 1979 and began teaching surgery at McGill University in 1987.

Over the past decade since I became a hospital and health-system director, my own role has evolved. I became president and CEO of the Integrated Health and Social Services University Network for West-Central Montreal in 2015. That experience informs my view that the evolution of healthcare described in this book can be a positive development if people understand it and take appropriate responsibility for themselves and others. I will be telling some dramatic stories that show why individuals will have to help their less technologically savvy friends and family, and policymakers will have to embrace a more holistic sense of healthcare delivery. We also will explore how our medical systems are being recognized as complex organizations that can address nonclinical health factors, such as nutrition and environment, with the aid of digitalization.

Human nature gives us comfort in the familiar and can blind us to changes that are happening in front of us. I remember sitting in my basement after dinner one night in 1994 showing relatives how I had home access to the internet earlier than most people because I was on the faculty at McGill University. They thought what I was doing online with this electronic mail system was ridiculous and would never catch on. Not surprisingly, one of their sons is in information technology today. The transformation of computing from mainframe to mainstream and its exponential growth in power are both a cause and a pattern for the emergence of a more people-centered healthcare system. People are being empowered with knowledge that allows all of us to take unprecedented personal responsibility for our health. The pages ahead will explain why personalized healthcare both empowers us and hands us new responsibilities we must all learn how to manage successfully.

CHAPTER 1

Healthcare Reborn: A Predictable, Unstoppable Disruption

Every January my son and I attend an international car show that takes over the convention center in Montreal, where I live. On our way to the show in 2020, riding in a taxi, I was struck by a feeling in the pit of my stomach that something was terribly wrong. When we passed through the Chinatown neighborhood, we saw many Asian people wearing masks like the ones I have worn as a surgeon. We had not seen anyone wearing masks earlier, but once we arrived at the convention center, we again remarked that almost all the Asian people at the car show were wearing masks, unlike anyone else. It struck me as unusual, so the next day at work I called a meeting with our health network's senior management team. "I think we have a problem," I said. It would be eight more weeks before the Canadian government woke up to the fact that they needed to counter a pandemic that inevitably would arrive in North America. But we could see from sporadic reports out of China that were not yet getting wide attention that we needed to prepare posthaste.

During the first wave of the COVID-19 pandemic, those of us in charge of facilities housing medically fragile populations knew we had to do something to protect both those we were caring for and our staff members. We didn't know what to expect from the new coronavirus in terms of possible contagion. The health network that I lead knew we had to innovate quickly, and we did so by working with Auger Groupe Conseil, a Microsoft development partner, to enable us to make virtual visits into rooms of our long-term care facilities.

In what could have been a scene in a science fiction film from not that many years ago, we used a type of hologram. The Microsoft HoloLens is a collaboration tool in which one person can do a mixed-reality visit that allows team members elsewhere to observe the scene without being in the same room. We achieved a major reduction in staff-to-resident contacts during a period when facilities such as ours were coping with outbreaks of the rapidly spreading virus, reducing transmission and the use of personal protective equipment. During a work shift in which one caretaker goes from room to room wearing a HoloLens, several doctors and nurses could have access as needed from their computer or tablet to interact with the patient. The mixed-reality device helped connect staff virtually and give seniors the attention of professionals, wherever they were. The technology not only addressed an immediate crisis but completely changed how we deal with people in long-term care. We continue to use the HoloLens and find additional applications for it. At the end of 2021, Microsoft Canada ranked our initiative one of its top-10 projects of the year.

This application of technology was an exceptional response to a crisis, but it also represents the general direction in which healthcare delivery was headed already. Knowledge is always evolving in medicine, but especially now processes are in motion involving various interdependent technologies that we need to understand and appreciate for their perceived disruptive nature.

The Decentralization Trend

To understand where we are in the emergence of a more personal healthcare system, consider how radically previous generations' centralization of computing has been reversed. Several decades ago, performing complicated calculations was largely an individual pursuit. I remember using a slide rule in my undergraduate physics class at McGill University in Montreal. I was among the first McGill students who requested we be allowed to use handheld electronic calculators, and we were told no, we could not. Mainframe computing that developed after World War II led to a centralization of computing. As a pre-med student learning a programming language called FORTRAN, I spent hours typing stacks of punch cards that I would carry to a computer center so they could be fed into mainframe computers that were purchased and maintained at huge cost by universities and other major institutions. The programming results could take hours or days, and if one character was typed incorrectly, the entire process had to be repeated. The expertise required to set up and maintain these machines was in very short supply well into the 1970s, when decentralization commenced. Computers became cheaper and started requiring far less intellectual and capital overhead. The introduction of desktop computers rapidly gave way to notebook computers, and more recently, the ever-present smartphone putting computing capacity with its attendant power and responsibility back into individual hands.

A similar, closely related historical arc has been transforming medicine. In the 20th century, the enormous expense and expertise required by new technology encouraged centralization. Diagnostic and treatment equipment was massive and difficult to maintain. It took a lot of smart people in one place to know how to use it and make it work, and those people were in short supply. Large medical centers as we know them emerged in North America after World War I. Some of these centers, such as Massachusetts General and Johns Hopkins, became renowned for their sophisticated abilities to diagnose and treat disease. I write about these institutions as a proud and appreciative insider. I earned my MD and my PhD in experimental surgery at McGill University in Montreal. As director of the Multi-Organ Transplant Program at Montreal General Hospital, I was able to inaugurate McGill's Pancreas Transplant Program and lead the team that performed the first successful liver transplant at McGill. The centralization produced amazing advances in lifesaving medicine and will continue to do so.

Toward the end of the 20th century and into the 21st century, technology became less expensive, smaller, and easier to transport and use. As a result, procedures that could be done only in a large medical center moved into community hospitals, then into clinics, and more recently into offices, strip malls, and people's living rooms. A related driver of the decentralization of medicine in recent years has been the ability of allied healthcare professionals to practice at a much higher level. General practitioners or family physicians could do something that only specialty physicians would do previously. Nurse practitioners, physician assistants, pharmacists, and other allied healthcare professionals stepped up to perform beyond their previous license.

This book will explain in much more detail how this evolution is occurring and what technology makes it an inevitable factor in the decentralization and disruption of the delivery of healthcare.

The Emergence of Connected Care

After realizing that we're all living through significant change, we should address the question, "Where do we go from here?" The prescription I will be providing in this book involves accepting the reality of emerging technology, encouraging the upscaling of people's abilities, and facilitating connected care that considers the social determinants of health (SDOH). The fact that technology is much more pervasive and easily used has led to what is called the democratization of technology. We are witnessing rapid developments in technologies, such as the internet of things, wearables, and remote sensing. Blockchain-based technology promises to help us meet challenges storing and distributing personal data while protecting individual privacy. Some readers may have enthusiastically embraced these technologies, and others may find them perplexing or disturbing, but they are in plain sight, and taken all together are used by hundreds of millions of people. All the largest retailers sell devices such as the Apple Watch, which can collect the wearer's health and fitness data and transmit it wirelessly. Self-administered blood-pressure cuffs in drugstores, big-box stores, and homes also collect data wirelessly. Companies such as Apple and Amazon that measure their value at a trillion US dollars have a stake in expanding this connected-care market. We all have lived through many changes to our lives and society due to the internet, so we should not expect healthcare delivery to be any less dynamic.

I attended a meeting in 2018 in Minneapolis at the US operational headquarters of a global medical instruments company, Medtronic. Well, at least I thought of it as a medical instruments company until the coffee break, when a staff member helped me navigate the route to the nearest washroom. We passed through a vast space filled with cubicles—individual computer workstations. "What is all this?" I asked. The Medtronic staffer explained it was a call center full of nurses. "What are you talking about? You're a medical equipment business," I replied. In fact, I learned that the company I knew for producing technology for robotic-assisted and minimally invasive surgery also was a medical services business. It was handling telehealth calls for six million VA patients, veterans who get medical services from the US Department of Veterans Affairs. Advances in remote monitoring and virtual visits made it feasible for a medical instrument company to expand into healthcare delivery.

Those of us who run academic medical centers also have a stake in these technologies because they make it less expensive and more convenient to care for patients. Bringing someone into a hospital involves a lot of overhead costs even before the person reaches the facility's skilled providers and expensive equipment, such as CT scanners. Someone pays to maintain the parking lot, the reception desk, and the waiting areas. Getting data from a sensor worn at home that used to require a trip to a diagnostic laboratory is the wave of the future. Everything that can be digitized will be digitized. The only uncertainties involve how we implement systems to make the technology as reliable, effective, and secure as possible.

Next-Generation Healthcare

The tremendous international research initiative over the past few decades to decipher and sequence the human genome is fundamentally changing the practice of medicine. It has rapidly led from an era of intuitive medicine through empirical medicine to what is being called personalized or precision medicine. As individual genomes are deciphered and sequenced, as we gain the ability to learn what's in our DNA, healthcare knowledge becomes democratized. It becomes the property of the patients to whom those genomes belong. This brings us to the concept of disintermediation, which we will explore in detail in chapter 8.

WHAT IS DISINTERMEDIATION?

At its most basic level, disintermediation simply eliminates an intermediary. We see this happening due to technology in our lives all the time without thinking much about it. Instead of brokers investing our money for us or travel agents arranging our vacation, we can go online and do it ourselves. Disintermediation and the democratization of knowledge go hand in hand. We can choose our investments or flight and hotel ourselves because online tools allow us to see and compare what's available. Brokers and travel agents still exist for the people and situations that call for intermediaries. Special knowledge retains value because democratization of knowledge is never complete. Every intermediary system has stakeholders who may resist or try to reverse disintermediation if doing so serves their personal, organizational, or financial interests. Those stakeholders could be agents, brokers, companies, institutions, or governments. This book will show how the disintermediation of healthcare affects stakeholders, such as academic medical centers, specialist physicians, and government policymakers.

Those threatened by disintermediation and the democratization of knowledge almost certainly face the uncomfortable realization that it is time to rethink their roles. In healthcare delivery, trying to deny or resist disintermediation is especially futile because behemoth companies, including Apple, Google, and Amazon, are coming in very quickly. We have seen how little control government exercises in regulating those big players. The field will be reconfigured, and we must reimagine our place and strategy. This book is meant as a resource for understanding what is happening and exploring the consequences of our responses.

The explanation of what is happening is as complex as the systems in which we deliver and pay for healthcare, which can seem almost chaotic. The allocations of costs among the public and private sectors vary by nation, and in North America by state or province, and they also vary by employment and age, among other factors. The ability and sustainability of delivering good results is precarious. Many nations have aging populations, which not only increases the health-care burden but contributes to staffing shortages. The World Health Organization in a 2019 report projected a shortfall of 18 million health workers to accelerate universal health coverage by 2030, particularly in low- and lower-middle-income countries.[1] A lot of money has been sunk into facilities and equipment whose purpose is being undermined by cheaper, smaller, more accurate diagnostic tools, some self-administered at home.

Let's Get Personal

The march of technology has made healthcare more of a personal responsibility than it has been since a couple of centuries ago, before our centralized medical establishment emerged. People can get insight

---

1   World Health Organization, "Addressing the 18 million health worker shortfall — 35 concrete actions and 6 key messages," who.int, published May 28, 2019, https://www.who.int/news/item/28-05-2019-addressing-the-18-million-health-worker-shortfall-35-concrete-actions-and-6-key-messages

into their health with the click of a button in ways that were not possible 10 years ago. There's no reason why everyone shouldn't take ownership of their body, their life, and their health. The ultimate extension of the decentralization of where care takes place and who provides the care is when it happens in your own living room. The trend points toward fewer people being seen in hospitals, maybe with a majority never being admitted to one.

Studies aimed at controlling our ever-rising healthcare costs have made clear that a lot of disease could be prevented if people had more information and could act upon it to lead a healthier lifestyle.[2] Social determinants, including poverty; health behaviors, such as diet and exercise; and lack of access to preventive care probably make up 80 percent to 90 percent of what determines the cost of healthcare.[3] High-end hospitals share in this cost but pay very little attention to preventing it because that work is not part of their mission. That situation is changing through the networking of health and social services.

Almost eight years ago as I write this, I was appointed as the president and CEO of the Integrated Health and Social Services University Network for West-Central Montreal. When I took that job, I had to stop practicing surgery and develop a more holistic

> **Technology has made healthcare more of a personal responsibility than it has been since a couple of centuries ago.**

---

2   Sanne Magnan, "Social Determinants of Health 101 for Health Care: Five Plus Five," discussion paper, NAM Perspectives (October 9, 2017), https://doi.org/10.31478/201710c.

3   Carlyn M. Hood, Keith P. Gennuso, Geoffrey R. Swain, and Bridget B. Catlin, "County Health Rankings: Relationships between Determinant Factors and Health Outcomes," American Journal of Preventive Medicine 50, iss. 2 (October 30, 2015): 129–35, https://doi.org/10.1016/j.amepre.2015.08.024.

perspective on healthcare delivery. Although the hub of that health network is a university hospital, it's a full-service health system offering a continuum of care on 34 sites. These sites include rehabilitation institutes, long-term care, mental health, community clinics, and palliative care facilities addressing a range of community health needs. In my previous job as chief of surgical services and later executive director of the Jewish General Hospital, I didn't really see the full scope of how healthcare delivery in the community was organized—or not organized—and how it was tracked and funded. Now I have the perspective to understand what is novel and the significance of the changes because of my long history in healthcare delivery.

As we connect the dots in this book between the developments in technology and healthcare delivery, it will be apparent that not everything is happening everywhere at the same pace. Some of my observations and experiences in Canada are in sync with parts of Europe but are probably still in the future for much of the United States. In chapter 9, we discuss why the US system is not sustainable the way it is configured, and for the Canadian system to be sustainable, it most likely will have to evolve by adapting policies and practices more like what's now seen in the US and Europe.

Human interaction will remain an important facet of healthcare delivery, just delivered less often by a doctor in a white coat and in less centralized settings. A nurse practitioner may provide care that is as good or better than the doctor's and at considerably less cost. This scenario already may be familiar to some readers but is in the early stages elsewhere. There always will be people resistant to the changes that come with digitalization, but change is coming to healthcare delivery just as it has in so many other industries, such as banking, travel, and the publishing and sale of books and periodicals.

Circling Back

In healthcare, as in computing, we went from a time when it was usually a very local, personal endeavor to it being a job that experts performed in centralized facilities staffed and maintained at great expense. The trend reversed, and we're moving back to a decentralized system. Healthcare delivery is evolving in parallel with the rapid development of technology that is usable by more people in more places. This democratization of medical technology and information requires those of us working in medical centers and as physicians and specialists to reimagine our roles and recognize the upscaling of our colleagues' and patients' abilities. Healthcare is becoming more of a personal responsibility; big technology companies are getting into the act and the emergence of connected care is changing the face of healthcare delivery. Decentralization can lower the cost of care because large academic medical systems are very expensive to maintain. But a lot of smart decisions must be made to ensure we can sustain the high-level specialized care some patients need.

Because humans and the systems we create connect with each other in complex ways, knowledge and practices are spread through networks. The stories I recounted of seeing people wearing surgical-type masks in Chinatown in January 2020 and how that observation eventually led to a hospital project involving a Microsoft collaboration technology shows how interdependent elements can coevolve. The next chapter will explain how and why that coevolution happens in systems and networks.

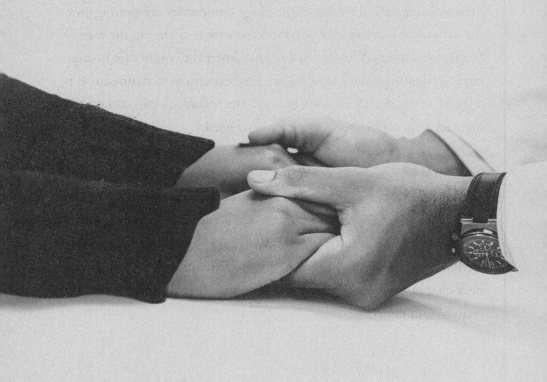

CHAPTER 2

Understanding the Complexity of Systems and Networks

You may know of the Cleveland Clinic as one of the world's top hospitals. But that well-deserved reputation overshadows another important story, as related to me by a fellow surgeon Toby Cosgrove, who was president and CEO of the Cleveland Clinic from 2004 to 2017. As the hospital grew into a huge campus it also became a sort of mother ship. The Cleveland Clinic began buying up medical practices around Ohio and adjacent states because of what we will explain is the only sustainable model for delivering healthcare—a network system. Cosgrove and his leadership team began to realize there was a reputational risk in buying up practices and putting a Cleveland Clinic label on them: patients would expect to receive care that was as good as being in the flagship hospital. So, the next logical step was to implant the high standards of the Cleveland Clinic into these practices by deploying doctors there from the mother ship.

That deployment approach was successful to a point, but not sustainable because it began depopulating the mother ship. The Cleveland Clinic had to restore its ranks by creating its own medical school, training the kind of people it wanted in the way it wanted them trained. I hadn't realized when I heard this story how the huge Cleveland Clinic network grew organically, but it resonated with me. Nearly a thousand kilometers northeast of Cleveland, I was executive director and CEO of Jewish General Hospital, a freestanding, independent teaching hospital affiliated with McGill University in Montreal. Then one day in 2015, the Quebec government blew up the provincial healthcare system, firing every hospital CEO in the province and disbanding the hospital boards of directors. The goal was to reconfigure all these previously independent organizations into integrated health networks.

Instead of having the health network evolve organically, as in Ohio, this was a top-down imposition by the Quebec government. I reapplied for my job running Jewish General Hospital, but instead of overseeing a freestanding hospital, I became CEO of a network. The healthcare and social service network now includes 34 sites as the result of the fusion of 10 previously independent organizations. What happened in Quebec in 2015 was much more disruptive than having a network bubble up gradually, as occurred in Ohio. But I can defend Quebec policymakers because the independent hospitals typified the much-maligned "silo" model of doing business. They didn't share information, leading to duplication, errors, and things falling between the cracks.

The only way to deliver efficient, holistic healthcare is with a network system dedicated to integrating a continuum of care across a defined population. Many parts of the world deliver care that way, but even where it is less common, such as in the United States, some large health systems have evolved organically. Typically, they are not government-imposed but materialize out of an existing need and the ingenuity and creativity of those partnering to form the network. Health maintenance organizations (HMOs), such as Kaiser Permanente in California, formed an early version of networks to care for patients. The networks evolving now are more sophisticated and holistic. To return to my Quebec example, the province has put healthcare and social services together under one ministry, reflecting the overwhelming role social determinants play in our health. Neighboring Ontario is considering the same consolidation.

To understand how and why healthcare networks evolve—and will continue to do so—requires some grounding in complexity theory. This chapter looks at the why, the what, and the how of complex systems developing for the delivery of healthcare through networks. We will delve briefly into theory to provide solid grounding for understanding what is happening in the real world in hospitals, clinics, pharmacies, and anywhere people deal with the health concerns of themselves or others.

Let's Start with Complexity Science

If the term "complexity science" had an agreed-upon definition, I would cite it here. Instead, let's suppose I asked every reader of this book to go look up the term. The results would be unpredictable, although discernable patterns would emerge in the definitions you found. Many of you might do an online search, and what you extracted would depend on your search terms, the algorithm of the search engine, which of the results you chose to open and read, and the knowledge and experience you brought to this research effort.

Some of you might spend a lot of time and effort developing a deep understanding of complexity science. Others might just ask a knowledgeable friend for a definition or team up with other readers to study the matter, in which cases human interactions would affect the results. The *complexity* I have just described stems partly from the fact that I did not lay out step-by-step rules each reader should follow in seeking a definition—a linear approach.

Someone who is trying to fix a car, find out why a computer crashed, or diagnose a common illness can follow a linear approach based on known cause-and-effect relationships. But healthcare is what complexity science calls a "complex adaptive system." Many components of the system have complex rules, but the challenge of complexity in healthcare results from the unpredictable and paradoxical ways that individual agents interact within a constantly changing system. A game in which new players keep arriving and making up their own rules is different from a game that has complex rules. Poor teamwork, miscommunications, and other failures in medical settings can have devastating effects, so a lot of study has gone into using complexity science to understand and improve health systems. What follows is a quick sampling of the research literature.

A game in which new players keep arriving and making up their own rules is different from a game that has complex rules.

"A complex adaptive system is a collection of individual agents with freedom to act in ways that are not always totally predictable, and whose actions are interconnected so that one agent's actions change the context for other agents."[4] With the resulting unpredictability, the only way to know what a complex system will do is to observe it and its overall patterns of behavior. Leaders instinctively want to trouble-shoot and resolve the complexity of healthcare issues.[5] "But complexity science suggests that it is often better to try multiple approaches and let direction arise by gradually shifting time and attention towards those things that seem to be working best."[6]

A report on a 2003 conference on applying complexity science to healthcare contained this comparison of organizational system characteristics:

COMPLEX ADAPTIVE SYSTEMS ...	TRADITIONAL SYSTEMS ...
are living organisms	are machines
are unpredictable	are controlling and predictive
are adaptable and flexible	are rigid and self-preserving
tap creativity	control behavior
embrace complexity	find comfort in control
evolve continuously	recycle

This report found that managers within complex adaptive systems have limited influence on change processes and must learn to flow with the change.[7]

---

4   Paul E. Plsek and Trisha Greenhalgh, "The Challenge of Complexity in Health Care," The BMJ (September 2001) 323, 625.

5   (Plsek and Trisha Greenhalgh, 627).

6   B. J. Zimmerman, C. Lindberg, and P. E. Plsek, Edgeware: Complexity Resources for Healthcare Leaders (Irving, TX: VHA Publishing, 1998), 263.

7   Center for the Study of Healthcare Management, Carlson School of Management, University of Minnesota, "Applying Complexity Science to Health and Healthcare," Publication 3 Series, March 2003, 5.

A research journal article noted that healthcare systems' control mechanisms must account for the unpredictability inherent in complex systems, recognizing that redundancy, flexibility, and enhanced communication are natural features of complex systems.[8]

The traditional hierarchical leadership structure is not a good way to envision or influence what's happening in a complex adaptive system. The interaction of different agents learning from and affecting each other is better represented in the model of a network.

Systems and Health Networks

I mentioned in chapter 1 that the systems in which we deliver and pay for healthcare can seem "almost chaotic," and I believe that is true regardless of whether we look at those systems from the perspective of a provider, policymaker, or consumer. In my experience, a day in the life of a surgeon can be affected by actions taken or decisions made by any number of independent agents, from paramedics and nurses to insurance and pharmaceutical companies to administrative, clerical, and cleaning staff. Policymakers pursue their organizational or governmental priorities within a public health ecosystem constrained by cultural traditions and the competing aims of multiple stakeholders. As consumers, we are used to simple linear systems in which we can easily compare the features and prices of products and

> **The only way to provide healthcare at the right time, at the right place, in the right way, to the right people is by recognizing that it is a network function.**

---

8   Mireya Martínez-García and Enrique Hernández-Lemus, "Health Systems as Complex Systems," *American Journal of Operations Research* 3 (January 2013): 113-126, https://dx.doi.org/10.4236/ajor.2013.31A011.

services, but the complexity in healthcare makes that kind of shopping around difficult, if not impossible.

Many systems are in place to keep the healthcare marketplace from descending into chaos. The amount of disagreement and uncertainty is held in check by what some refer to as "systemness." In my world, this notion means effectively integrating healthcare in multiple locations. The only way to provide healthcare at the right time, at the right place, in the right way, to the right people is by recognizing that it is a network function. The decentralization we discussed in chapter 1 has spurred the creation of networks, as in the Cleveland Clinic example, and made the 20th century's hierarchical, top-down leadership models obsolete. Complexity science teaches us networks emerge when multiple interdependent elements organically coevolve. To put that concept in everyday language, networks tend to bubble up from the bottom and are rarely imposed from above, notwithstanding my 2015 experience in Quebec.

This network theory presupposing that change is organic and not dictated from the top down begs the question of what role policymakers have in shaping the healthcare disruption. Whatever political party is in power is much more likely to set boundaries than drive change. Constrained by political systems and budgetary considerations, policymakers must align their hopes and plans to the reality of what is emerging organically—when or if they understand what is happening. Given how rapid the digital transformation has been, it's not surprising that laws, regulations, and policies lag years behind in adapting. The horizon of an upcoming election can make it impossible to propose changes that are expensive or potentially controversial.

Political and Business Players

A president or prime minister may set out to impose a top-down approach to adapting health systems, only to realize that nongovernmental actors already have shaped the arena. Four types of companies are reacting very quickly to the evolving landscape of healthcare delivery:

Lean innovators: Most people are aware of companies that are applying cutting-edge science and technology to produce pharmaceuticals, devices, and digital products that help people to improve their health and manage their diseases.

Pharma services: Large pharmaceutical companies, such as Switzerland's Roche and Novartis, have divisions that provide solutions and services to supplement their drug business.

Value innovators: Companies that have the resources to perform large-scale healthcare delivery in efficient new ways are getting into the field regardless of whether it was their traditional mission. We saw that in the story in chapter 1 about Medtronic, one of the largest medical-instrument companies in the world, branching into medical services with its VA call-center contract.

Digital innovators: Apple, Amazon, and Google will increasingly be very involved in healthcare delivery, as will the blockchain companies. Blockchain technology allows data that currently resides in healthcare centers and doctors' offices to be stored and retrieved from anywhere and encrypted so it can be kept private and validated.

The initiatives by Apple, Amazon, and Google—companies that once had nothing to do with healthcare—are prima facie evidence that what's going on is not being driven from the top down by government policymakers. For ordinary healthcare consumers, the emerging changes transform their role in a positive way, giving them skin in the game. They may feel less like passive recipients or victims of a system as they gain more understanding of digital innovations and how to use them in their favor. Similar understanding is crucial for healthcare professionals and students pursuing such careers, as their training must prepare them for their evolving functions. Medical training can have a long horizon—10 years for a specialist physician. Given the speed at which technology is changing, these doctors should not expect to end up with the role they thought they were going to have when they entered medical school. They should not be surprised that chatter they hear today about 5G phones, the metaverse, and blockchain reflect real forces predictably shaping how they will interact with colleagues and patients.

Depending on where you live, change may come slower or faster. Some countries have government more involved; others, such as the United States, have more private enterprise controlling healthcare. Technology is more advanced, obviously, in some places, but its development can make surprising leaps. In parts of Africa, for example, where telecommunications infrastructure lagged far behind more developed countries, investment skipped directly into cellular technology. Adoption of wireless phones happened faster than in countries with older populations reliant on landlines. Because the technology jumped a generation, it is probably more advanced than in many Western countries. Japan, which has an aging population and a shortage of workers, has leaped ahead in reliance on robotic technology—robots delivering services in long-term care residences and acting as home health aides. Once such an adaptation happens, it inevitably spreads to similar areas, such as Florida or Quebec, which both have older populations. Culturally, it's easy to depict robots as something to fear, and we can envision elderly patients struggling to adapt to new technology. But people adapt with the help of their families and institutional support, and the result is nothing to fear.

Individual Empowerment

Decentralization and disintermediation in healthcare delivery shift power, control, and knowledge outward from specialist physicians and siloed academic medical centers. People gain more control over how they interact with the system and what's done to them and by whom. Dr. Eric Topol envisioned this optimistic scenario in a 2015 book, *The Patient Will See You Now: The Future of Medicine Is in Your Hands.* He wrote that medicine was coming to a "Gutenberg moment," like the way the printing press took learning to the masses. But instead of printed books being the mechanism, it's our mobile phones facilitating self-diagnosis. Many healthcare providers were alarmed or at least unhappy when patients first started using Google to look up their symptoms, resulting in a lot of time wasted correcting patients' mistaken conclusions. But over the years people got better at using the internet, and many patients come in as well-informed or better informed than their physicians about what is happening to their bodies.

THE CASE OF THE WELL-INFORMED PATIENT

Antibiotics are arguably the most abused medication in the history of pharmacology. For years, many doctors prescribed antibiotics to anybody who came in with a cough or a sore throat when most of those illnesses were caused by a virus. The doctors knew, or should have known, that antibiotics were useless against a virus, and their overuse would contribute to antibiotic resistance, which became a huge problem. The medical establishment blamed the patients for insisting on being given a pill when no antiviral was available. The ability of patients to get reliable medical information on demand anywhere and anytime makes it much more likely they will know when an antibiotic is indicated.

The disintermediation in primary care means it makes no sense to provide it in a hospital environment, as happens so often by default in many places. Research at Harvard Business School led by Professor Michael E. Porter[9] pointed to the need for a strategy to maximize value to patients by achieving the best outcomes and the lowest costs by having providers concentrate the care for each of the conditions they treat in the right locations. This concept of system integration starts by determining the overall scope of services a provider can effectively deliver, then choosing the right location for each service. In essence, these integrated units are a network system. Some jurisdictions around the world have imposed network systems, but others have grown organically over decades. What is now known as Kaiser

---

9   Michael E. Porter and Thomas H. Lee, "The Strategy That Will Fix Health Care," Harvard Business Review, October 2013, https://hbr.org/2013/10/the-strategy-that-will-fix-health-care.

Permanente traces its roots to a 12-bed California hospital built in the Mojave Desert during the Great Depression. It now serves more than 12 million Americans. The world's second-largest HMO after Kaiser, Clalit Health Services in Israel, emerged from the labor movement in 1911, long before the State of Israel was founded in 1948. In both cases, the original intent was to care for workers, but the mission greatly expanded to meet changing needs.

We must encourage the public to educate or reeducate themselves to function effectively in this evolving healthcare landscape. Everyone involved in healthcare delivery must learn or relearn how and when to escalate levels of treatment from primary care to the secondary care of specialists and the tertiary care provided in our more advanced hospitals. A colleague who is the CEO of a university-affiliated hospital has described that facility publicly as providing quaternary care, indicating it specializes in patients that need to go to the one place in the world that can deal with their highly unusual condition. The need to cover the high costs of extremely specialized care has led to world-class academic medical centers like the Cleveland Clinic buying up community practices to diversify their revenue.

The democratization of medical knowledge and technology changes the status and role of care providers. Family doctors, being better informed than ever, are increasingly in competition with specialist physicians. Nurse practitioners who have received the training and certification to practice at the top of their license also will be better informed than ever. The outflow of knowledge and information means that patients and whoever they get to see for treatment will be better prepared. But not everyone embraces the inevitable disruption because it threatens to remove control of the healthcare delivery process from those who oversee it. Keeping control of the process is not only a political power play but also allows them to keep control of the money at a time when huge tech companies are circling the field. Some of their motivation no doubt stems from those companies' business interest in obtaining as much data as they can about everyone. But they also can make important contributions. The tech companies, with their data-processing abilities and artificial intelligence (AI), can backstop medical institutions that have a worsening shortage of skilled people. With their skill at marketing wellness and fitness devices, like wristwatches that measure the oxygen saturation of the user's blood, the tech companies may give a boost to the preventive medicine that would lower our costs of treating chronic disease.

Circling Back

While the business world has long recognized the drawbacks of individuals or departments operating in their own silos, this concept has not penetrated medicine to the same extent. The traditional, free-standing hospital or medical center can be a quintessential silo. A more naturally occurring healthcare system would deal with issues across the continuum of care, as opposed to just episodic, acute diagnosis and treatment. But the decentralization and digitalization trends we discussed in chapter 1 are pushing healthcare into a network structure. In the business world, technology innovations that significantly change an industry are labeled as disruptive. People working in healthcare see changes disrupting their routines and even in some cases threatening their livelihoods, but it would be an oversimplification to call what's happening a disruption. From a systems point of view, what's unfolding is a natural evolution of ecosystems. This chapter covered the theoretical explanation of why and how that move is happening. In the pages ahead, we look deeper into where technology-driven change is leading healthcare.

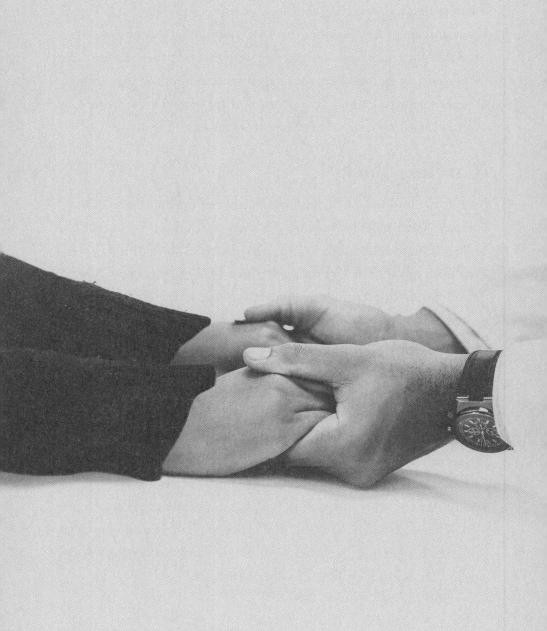

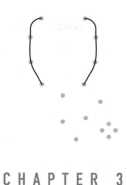

CHAPTER 3

Digitalization and Real-Time Health Systems

During the COVID-19 pandemic, numerous people were told for the first time *not* to visit a doctor or hospital for a serious illness but to monitor their condition at home. I'll take you behind the scenes of that dramatic shift to help explain the role of digitalization in the reshaping of healthcare delivery.

The omicron variant of the coronavirus produced a wave of people testing positive for COVID in December 2021, but in Montreal we did not see a notable increase in hospitalizations until mid-January 2022. As a hospital administrator, I found it reassuring that the length of stay for those patients was a lot shorter than for people who had been admitted during the first or second wave of the pandemic. To have enough beds for our COVID patients back then, we had to dramatically reduce elective surgery, a drastic measure because diseases can worsen, surgeries can get more complicated, and patients can be left suffering in pain when nonemergency surgery is delayed. As the omicron wave peaked, I called a huddle of our senior managers on a Friday morning to find a way to keep the surgical program running. By Monday morning, we had created a program to look after COVID patients at home, including providing them oxygen and monitoring them around the clock.

Services existed to provide people with chronic respiratory conditions oxygen at home, but nobody in Canada had ever tried to set up such a program for an acute condition like COVID. Our team worked almost without sleep for 72 hours to make it happen. The omicron patients typically needed oxygen for a limited time, and we didn't want to take up hospital beds figuring out how long of a time that would be in each case. We thought if we could deliver oxygen to their homes and monitor their use of that oxygen in real time, along with all important vital signs, we could prevent admissions or, when COVID patients were hospitalized, get them out several days sooner. With beds filling up, there was no time for the usual cautious but bureaucratic process through which medical advances and initiatives are reviewed and approved.

Before the pandemic, we had done some planning about how to set up a hospital-at-home program. We pulled the plans off the shelf, contacted oxygen suppliers, and shopped for monitoring devices that would not involve work on the patient's side. We could teach a patient or family member to snap an oximeter onto a finger to check oxygen levels, but patients can't keep those devices on and check them around the clock, whether they are bedridden or feeling well enough to move around their home. We wanted a device ordinary people could just slap onto their chest to transmit a continuous signal over Wi-Fi to be monitored on a computer screen in our health-care network's pandemic command center. It turned out that such a product was not yet commercially available in Canada. But an Israeli digital health technology company, Maisha-Labs, with whom we had worked to stand up the command center, introduced us to yet another Israeli company, Biobeat, which produced disposable wearables. These devices were initially available in limited supply, and as the number of patients increased, we put in an urgent order for more to be shipped by courier. We issued smartphones with the monitoring devices to ensure data was transmitted to the cloud in a secure, reliable way for monitoring in real time 24/7 in the command center.

I knew that the team members organizing this effort, our ever-resilient cardiology chief and our tenacious associate director of quality, would set up strict safety protocols to exclude any patients they might see as being at risk in the hospital-at-home program. I warned then that if the exclusion criteria were too strict, we would end up with no participants. Sure enough, on Monday morning I found out we had nobody to put into the program. All the candidates were too old, too sick, too reluctant, not tech-savvy, etc. The solution to this problem was right in front of me on my office wall, where I had one of those motivational plaques paraphrasing a famous quote from the late American football coach Vince Lombardi, saying, "Perfection is not attainable, but if we chase perfection, we can catch excellence." I invoked a version of the Pareto principle, or 80/20 rule: if we could find the best 20 percent of the candidates, no matter how imperfect, we could get 80 percent of what we wanted done accomplished. In the end, the program met its goals.

Connected and Real-Time Healthcare

Connected healthcare is the ability to monitor signals from anywhere at any time from anybody to collect data needed to make medical decisions. The result of connected healthcare technology is that it enables a real-time health system (RTHS) in ways we have never seen before, with the individual being the owner of the data and in control of his or her wellness.

Technology has a way of making new connections and finding new use cases. Our hospital-at-home program planned to include only patients in our service area, but cloud computing technology allowed us to drop that exclusion, and the first several participants were from outside our territory. Our Jewish General Hospital's connection to Maisha-Labs started several years earlier when we were shopping for cybersecurity defense technology. Undoubtedly, their help in getting Biobeat's usage approved by Health Canada regulators was invaluable and would eventually permit the supplier to expand its market. As a startup, Biobeat had sought to use data science and AI to monitor stress and mental well-being, but its noninvasive wearable technology found a new use in the pandemic. The interconnectedness that these devices enable is so typical of how the system is unfolding.

There are a lot of unintended interdependencies created that emerge, as would be expected, in the context of complexity and complex adaptive systems. When we first began working with Maisha-Labs, it was initially just as it relates to cybersecurity. Then we worked with them to develop the command center, which expanded our reach when the pandemic hit. And when we wanted to set up our hospital-at-home program, we relied on them for the appropriate technology—the wearables. This brought us to Biobeat. From there, we worked with Maisha-Labs to help Biobeat go through the Health Canada approval process for the device.

Since nobody wanted patients sitting in crowded waiting rooms during the pandemic, virtual doctor visits proliferated. That gave a boost to another Israeli company that produces the TytoCare Medical Exam Kit. The kit facilitates virtual doctor visits by giving patients an exam camera and digital devices to put in their ear and throat, to take their blood pressure and temperature, and listen to their lungs and heart. The doctor or other care provider can receive the results in real time during a video call. Patients obviously have a learning curve, just as they did in adopting smartphones, but several health systems have reported high acceptance and satisfaction with the results.

Increasingly common network-enabled devices, which some call the internet of things, are enabling our healthcare networks in new ways all the time. The change is happening so fast I enrolled in a 10-week online course on connected care at McMaster University in Ontario—back-to-school time for a 67-year-old, tenured professor at McGill University. Applying AI and machine learning to data can change everything we think we understand about healthcare. While attending a cybersecurity and healthcare conference in Germany, I was amazed and alarmed to learn it was possible to hack into a hospital information network through a CT or MRI scanner. European experts at the conference showed that, in theory, once they broke into the network, malefactors could kill someone by remotely changing the settings on a respirator. Enterprise administrators and law-enforcement officials are locked in a struggle to stay ahead of threats like these. We cannot underestimate the unintended consequences of digitalization even beyond incidents like the ransomware attacks that we have seen happening.

For the average person, connected care manifests itself as a convenience, not a threat. For example, electronic medical records allow different providers to share data, which can prevent unnecessary testing, treatment delays, or the dangerous mixing of drugs. Your family physician can see you received a vaccine from a pharmacist, and all of you can see that you are due for a booster shot. In a real-time healthcare system, the doctor would get a notification, "Mary Jones just got her COVID booster." Of course, physicians wouldn't put up with the intrusion of such messages pouring into their smartphones 24 hours a day. AI must come into play to distinguish important signals and route all the notifications appropriately. With electronic access, patients gain visibility into the data and observations their providers have recorded about them, enabling them to prevent errors and clear up misunderstandings about care and billing. Patients increasingly demand healthcare networks offer transparency in pricing and the routine conveniences consumers have come to expect from other businesses, such as online scheduling, evening or weekend hours, and nearby locations.

As digital devices get smaller, cheaper, more mobile, more functional, and easier to use, connected healthcare moves functions out of large medical centers. We have digitalized and miniaturized diagnostic equipment that used to be so large and expensive it had to be in a hospital or in some other centralized facility staffed by experts. Some of the equipment is now in the homes and hands of the patient. Of course, it's also in the hospitals, where we have robotic surgery, wearable monitors, and wireless computers on wheels that we call COWs. Miniaturization sometimes is limited in an institutional setting by practical considerations: Staff members don't want to stare at small screens all day or night, and handheld devices bring issues with ergonomics and battery life. But when we compare the medical functionality of home and hospital versions, bigger is not necessarily better.

Connected Care Requires Teamwork

I received a white paper on creating a community of connected care from Optum, Inc., a large US health-services company, that did an excellent job explaining what it called "a whole-health approach" in which a team fully supports the individual:

> Connected care links information, insight, services and the principles of holistic health across a network of diverse partners to drive timely, health-giving actions in any locale. In this approach, payers, providers, employers and the community each have a role to play and a distinct service to perform. But instead of any singular entity "owning the relationship," the collective works together. They have an agreed-upon standard of service and share responsibility for the well-being of the whole person.
>
> People spend significantly more time in their community than in the health system. Health organizations can start collaborating with community organizations to develop human-centered processes that screen for a more holistic set of needs. A connected care team is continually assessing for needs as people move through their community and can guide people to the right resources when they need them.[10]

---

10   Optum, Inc., "Connected Care: Seeing the Whole Picture for Whole-Person Health," July 2022, 10.

Four tenets set the foundation for the whole-health approach, the Optum contributing experts wrote:

- Physical and behavioral health are connected—one impacts the other.
- Social drivers of health, community, and family have a profound impact on health engagement.
- Personal goals motivate behavior more than health goals.
- Care and support must be able to serve people regardless of their physical location.

Digital Leapfrogging

Digitalization provides tools for those people who want more control over their own healthcare to make it more patient driven. They can gain more access to care and more timely care by being early adopters of whatever the internet of things offers. Other patients and providers will hold off until they have no choice but to make a technological leap. Once AI is layered in on top of the data that comes from connected care, the RTHS will achieve better decision making and a reduction in care variation, which will lead to more cost-effective care and less waste. These intermediate- to longer-term benefits eventually will promote wide adoption faster in some places than in others. In the previous chapter, we discussed how technology responds to cultural, demographic, and geographic situations and can skip ahead a generation in one place or another. Japan's aging population created a need for home-care robots, and

> **Digitalization provides tools for those people who want more control over their own healthcare to make it more patient driven.**

Africa's lack of landline infrastructure sped adoption of cellular phones. Similar digital leapfrogging is inevitable in healthcare delivery.

THE ESTONIA EXAMPLE

The most digitally advanced healthcare system in the world is in the northern European country of Estonia. It is a universal healthcare system in which everyone has a blockchain account to secure their medical information. Five years after gaining independence from the Soviet Union, Estonia joined the European Union in 2004, and its economy developed rapidly. Estonia invested in technology education and leapt ahead of much larger countries in computer programming and enabling people to study, work, and vote online. Estonian programmers designed and implemented a sophisticated, secure system for healthcare delivery. It uses virtual reality to an extent that would surprise health policymakers elsewhere.

As with everything, somebody needs to pay for the advances in digitalization, and controlling costs requires good management. Setting standards and ensuring that the digital components are interoperable are huge challenges. Connected health requires that the various technologies involved can connect. Fortunately, the healthcare industry and government regulators recognized this challenge and began in 2012 to develop a Fast Healthcare Interoperability Resources (FHIR) standard for how digital information can be exchanged. The big tech companies came on board too. Still, enterprises like my health network have legacy software platforms that don't talk to each other, requiring duplicate work in collecting and retrieving patient information. In our case, the electronic healthcare records, the finance software, and the system that handles admissions, discharges, and transfers are not at all interoperable.

Healthcare systems have increasingly realized that the data they collect from patients should include SDOH. The fast-rising and overwhelming cost of treating chronic, preventable conditions has driven up interest among the governments and private insurers who pay for healthcare. People without adequate housing, reliable transportation, and social support and those living in neighborhoods where the only food sellers are convenience stores and fast-food restaurants are especially susceptible. A 2021 report by the US research outfit Insider Intelligence said SDOH initiatives are on the rise partly because of a shift to value-based care, a reimbursement model that pays providers based on the quality of care they deliver rather than the quantity of services they provide.[11] It noted that big tech was on board with this effort too: "Google is using its Healthcare API to help providers make better use of nonclinical info, Uber and Lyft are partnering with healthcare organizations to facilitate rides to appointments, and Amazon is using its Alexa voice assistant to help caregivers keep tabs on seniors from afar."

Patients come with their own data sources. Every doctor has a story of a patient coming in with a pile of printouts because they searched their symptoms on Google. Most doctors understandably have misgivings about spending time discussing the patient's research, but a better-informed patient is a better patient. The challenge in connected and real-time healthcare is to move patients who found a bottomless pit of information on the internet to a pool of useful knowledge. I wish I could tell you I have figured out how to get there.

---

11   Zoë LaRock, "The Social Determinants of Health," Insider Intelligence, published March 2021, https://www.insiderintelligence.com/content/the-social-determinants-of-health.

I hope that as the AI improves, it will help both physicians and patients triage the information that they're receiving.

The internet not only has misinformation, but it also has patients' personal data that should be confidential. On the dark web, a hidden part of the internet that facilitates anonymity, stolen medical information is more valuable than stolen credit card information because it can be used to commit insurance fraud. The issues of protecting data and securing systems against cyberattacks bring us back to the question of who controls and pays for our emerging decentralization and connectedness. For example,

> **When you can do the test yourself at home, who is paying for that service, how is the data securely entered into your digital medical records, and who owns that data?**

Canada has public funding of necessary medical care provided by hospitals and physicians, but several types of supplemental care, such as dental and vision, can be covered by the government, private health insurance, or out-of-pocket, depending on people's circumstances. As people take ownership of their healthcare by using home-based technology, control and cost coverage will have to be reconciled with the mix of provider-payer relationships. When you go to a hospital for a test, the hospital is responsible for both getting paid and securing the data. When you can do the test yourself at home, who is paying for that service, how is the data securely entered into your digital medical records, and who owns that data? Those questions deal with immediate and practical implications of the ways we will be discussing that connected and real-time healthcare already are beginning to affect all of us.

MY EXPERIENCE WITH CONNECTED CARE

As I was finishing the first draft of this book, I came down with COVID, and what happened next reinforced my belief in what I already had written in this chapter about connected care. The night of July 21, 2022, I developed a headache, a low-grade fever, and a little, funny, scratchy feeling in my throat. The next morning, I went to get tested at the hospital where I work, and I stayed at the office after I tested negative for COVID. As the morning rolled on, I got increasingly more pain in my throat. The headache went away, but by the next night, on Friday, I had a high temperature and pharyngitis so severe I couldn't eat or drink for five or six days. Forty-eight hours after initially testing negative, I retested, and that time did test positive.

Needing an intravenous infusion to stay hydrated, I entered the hospital-at-home program that I had helped start. And although my symptoms felt more horrible than I could have imagined, I was very happy to be in my own bed and not wasting a hospital bed just to have an IV.

In my firsthand experience, hospital at home lived up to its billing even after we encountered an unusual glitch. Someone from the hospital dropped off the equipment, and then a different person from our home-care team came to insert the intravenous line, which has an electric pump to ensure the recipient gets the right amount of liquid every hour. A couple of hours later, my part of the city had a power failure! Luckily, it lasted only about 30 minutes, and the pump has a three-hour battery backup. I remained in the hospital-at-home program for seven days. You might expect that the CEO would get extra care, but I got less than most people because I declined the 24-hour remote monitoring. I could monitor myself with the help of my wife, who is a nurse, and my familiarity with using my Apple Watch to measure vital signs. As noted previously, some individuals will always be better able than others to take advantage of connected-care technology. People may not have someone at home to help, or their housing situation may not be stable or accessible. The power outage brought home how programs must be flexible to deal with whatever complications arise. As healthcare becomes more personal and decentralized, we must innovate ways to extend connected care to everyone, including the most vulnerable.

Circling Back

This chapter looked at a variety of digitalization initiatives in healthcare—remote patient monitoring, virtual visits, interoperable data collection, AI screening of data, and paying more attention to SDOH. Healthcare services increasingly reach people where they are, sometimes with the help of startup or big tech companies. The ability to monitor signals from anywhere at any time from anybody creates a connected care system and enables an RTHS, which together are more patient centered than our traditional medical-center-based establishment. In the next chapter, we will take a deeper dive into the data available about individuals through advances in precision medicine.

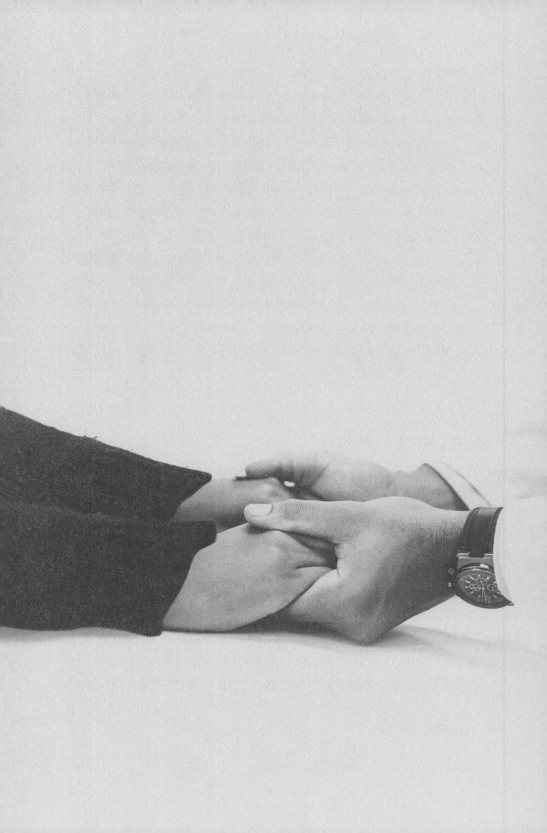

CHAPTER 4

Precision Medicine: Why It's Personal Now

The US Food and Drug Administration gave a health tech company, 23andMe, authorization in 2015 to market the first direct-to-consumer genetic test. The company had been around since 2006, performing laboratory analyses of saliva samples. Its customers are people who want to learn about their ancestry and genetic traits from their DNA. In the process, they might learn they carry bad genes or are predisposed to certain diseases, which is why public health officials got involved. In 2013, the FDA informed 23andMe that the company's at-home testing kits were medical devices requiring regulatory approval. Few would argue with the federal agency's stated aims to assess whether the tests were accurate and valid, meaning they could reliably measure what they claim to measure and predict what they say they can predict. But the way regulation of direct-to-consumer genetic testing has played out, regulation seems to be standing in the way of the emerging disintermediation and democratization of healthcare.

As 23andMe developed its testing to assess genetic risks for more diseases and conditions, it had to overcome new regulatory hurdles. The FDA was selective in what genetic information it decided needed safeguarding. Genetic testing can reveal many interesting but sometimes trivial things about people and their bodily functions. The agency focused on what testing would reveal about serious conditions that require medical treatment. It took years for 23andMe to win approval to report risks of colorectal, prostate, and breast cancer. The FDA eventually approved the tests but warned they should not be used for diagnosis or to inform treatment decisions.

The FDA's approach struck me as paternalistic—the government stepping in as an arbiter of people's rights to know information about themselves from the emerging field of precision medicine. Consider the testing for genetic mutations related to breast cancer because that 2018 FDA approval got wide public attention. The genetic testing report from 23andMe covered mutations in the BRCA1 and BRCA2 genes, which are the most common in the Ashkenazi Jewish population, not the general population. Any customers of 23andMe who learned they had a high risk of developing breast cancer due to that gene sequence might choose to undergo prophylactic mastectomy, but the testing company was not telling them they should do so. Nobody was forcing anyone to become a customer of 23andMe if they had concerns that we will discuss later in the book about privacy or getting disturbing results. They didn't need a prescription to get the test, but it was up to the individual what results they chose to see and what to do with those results. They certainly needed to consult with a doctor to proceed with surgery or treatment.

Understanding Precision Medicine

The US National Institutes of Health defined precision medicine as "an emerging approach for disease treatment and prevention that takes into account individual variability in genes, environment, and lifestyle for each person."[12] It is emerging partly because science is giving us more knowledge of genetics and genomics every day. (For readers whose knowledge of biology is a bit hazy or dated, genetics is the study of hereditary characteristics and variations. Genomics is a branch of biotechnology involved in mapping and DNA sequencing of sets of genes.) The international gene mapping project exemplifies how the emergence of new uses from developing technology can be both evolutionary and revolutionary. Researchers first celebrated the sequencing of the human genome in 2001. Although the blueprint they published was only about 92 percent complete, the accomplishment enabled great progress in understanding the role of genetics in susceptibility to disease. Emerging technology allowed researchers to fill in the gaps over two decades and publish what they called a complete "human reference genome" at the end of March 2022.

Sequencing the human genome was not only a tremendous scientific feat for international researchers. It also enabled the evolution of healthcare we are discussing in this book—the democratization of knowledge and care and the empowerment of the individual. In precision medicine, healthcare providers use genetics and genomics to better understand disease and determine appropriate therapy. But that advance is only part of the story of the demise of what has often been derided as "one-size-fits-all medicine."

---

12   Garrido P, Aldaz A, Vera R, Calleja MA, de Álava E, Martín M, Matías-Guiu X, Palacios J, "Proposal for the creation of a national strategy for precision medicine in cancer," Clinical & Translational Oncology, vol. 20, accessed December 15, 2022, 443-447, doi: 10.1007/s12094-017-1740-0.

The bigger picture we see in our healthcare networks is that we are amassing a tremendous amount of data from the connected and real-time healthcare we discussed in the previous chapter. A lot of that data is personal, involving not only the patient's physical condition and prescriptions but also the patient's history, lifestyle, and health behaviors and socioeconomic factors. Taking all this data into account, people have the power to become more engaged in their own decisions around their own health and wellness.

> **People have the power to become more engaged in their own decisions around their own health and wellness.**

Dramatic accounts about people dealing with revelations from genetic testing should not overshadow the more ordinary, everyday inroads that precision medicine is making in our lives. People who are seeing personal, real-time health data on their wristwatches are participants in precision medicine by and for themselves.

Geneticists and other medical specialists tend to discuss precision medicine in a different context. They'll tell you, for example, that genetic sequencing has allowed oncologists to see breast cancer as not one disease but many different diseases. Depending on the gene sequence, they can select a personalized chemotherapy or radiation strategy for a particular subtype of cancer. The development of molecular therapies and, more recently, immunotherapies targeted against genomic sequences of tumors is a great development worthy of the attention it has received. It also points to how much we have yet to learn about the genomic influences in the diseases we treat, especially psychiatric illness. These genomic influences and the social determinants of health are interrelated in a complex, patient-centered ecosystem in which one factor can give rise to another.

Emerging Personalized Medicine

Personalized medicine has been evolving for many decades. In 1948, the US Public Health Service began a study in Framingham, Massachusetts, to look at cardiovascular risk factors across a large population. The participants received physical examinations, and the researchers also collected information regarding diet, physical activity, depression, and social networks. The landmark study and many others that followed influenced how healthcare providers profile their patients.

McKinsey & Company consultants published a paper in June 2020 calling for an ecosystem-based, patient-centered model of healthcare.[13] The paper reflected my thinking and made the case in terms a business leader would appreciate. The authors used Disney as an example to explain how an ecosystem has components reinforcing each other. "Disney launched its first movie in 1937, its first television series in 1954, and, by 2019, the streaming service Disney+. Its theme parks, such as Disney World, reinforce the brands of characters, allowing children and families to have engaging in-person experiences. Those children also ask for Disney toys, Disney apparel, and Disney games, creating a self-reinforcing experience within the ecosystem enabled by the control of a scarce resource—content—and the underlying data and analytics to best deliver it." This metaphor captures how an ecosystem connects with people in different ways and different places. The consumer may be at home wearing a T-shirt depicting a Disney character or may travel to have an expensive interaction with flashy new technology.

---

13   Shubham Singhal, Basel Kayyali, Rob Levin, and Zachary Greenberg, "The Next Wave of Healthcare Innovation: The Evolution of Ecosystems," McKinsey & Company, June 23, 2020, https://www.mckinsey.com/industries/healthcare-systems-and-services/our-insights/the-next-wave-of-healthcare-innovation-the-evolution-of-ecosystems.

In the medical ecosystem, it has become technically feasible and financially affordable to do large-scale gene sequencing to begin to learn about the various genomic risks involved and understand disease at a molecular level. To put it simply, there was a time when doctors didn't really know why a treatment worked for one patient and not for another. Bad luck, maybe? Now they can recognize and target a patient's specific genetic mutations. Our knowledge has grown, but just as important, the process has become more affordable. Twenty years ago, doing a whole genome sequence cost $100 million. By 2012, the same process might have cost $5,000, and now the price tag is in the hundreds, meaning the evaluation can be done on an individual's cancer tissue sample, blood cells, or cheek-tissue swab.

Genetics and Personal Decisions

Awakened by a call in the middle of the night, I learned that my father had been admitted to Columbia Presbyterian Hospital in New York while on a business trip. This was in 1987 when I was learning transplant surgery during a fellowship at the University of Michigan in Ann Arbor. I rushed to fly to New York, but first I had to make a medical decision for my father. He was being offered an infusion, and he didn't have a clue what they were talking about in asking him to sign a consent form. Whoever woke me said, "Your father's here in the emergency room. He told us you're a doctor. Would you give us permission to infuse him with this new anticoagulation drug (tPA) that we're proposing to use in people with acute myocardial infarction?" I said yes, and my father became one of the first participants in a trial of an anticlotting therapy for heart attacks.

What I knew before making the medical decision was that serious heart disease ran in my father's side of the family as far back as I could be aware of. I never knew my paternal grandfather because he died at the age of 36, presumably of a sudden cardiac event. His brother suffered a similar death. My father was 56 when he showed up at the New York hospital. He recovered from that heart attack enough to live 16 more years but with eventually fatal heart disease. When my son was born, I was determined to be around to watch him grow up, so I figured I had better do whatever I could to counter my family's bad genes. Mindful that my father was somewhat overweight much of his life and smoked on and off, I was determined to be the poster boy for cardiac health, not smoking, having a good diet, and exercising regularly. But when I went to the cardiac risk assessment unit of the hospital where I was working and asked for a complete review, I found that doing everything I was supposed to do was not enough. My risk score index came back high because I couldn't control my genes.

Precision medicine came through for me and my family members when antistatin drugs became widely available for those of us with high cholesterol. It's a common story that extends to many diseases and conditions as precision medicine gives us the insight to take more control of our bodies and personal responsibility for our health. Just as I made decisions about not smoking, diet, and exercise based on knowledge of my family medical history, I think I should be able to decide to be informed about my genome sequence and any risks it points to. Perhaps the knowledge will help me make informed decisions not only about medical treatment but also about prevention and financial planning. In chapters 6 and 12, we will discuss the imperative for people to be educated on how to transform information into actionable insight.

"FROM PREWOMB TO TOMB"

Eric Topol, author of *The Patient Will See You Now*, wrote a 2014 journal article predicting that defining each individual's unique biology with genomics and other -omics will play an increasing role in medicine through our lifespans[14]. This is a simplified version of Topol's vision of the timeline.

- Before conception: genomic screening
- At 8–12 weeks of pregnancy: fetal blood test for chromosomal abnormalities and sex
- At birth: sequencing the genome of the newborn to rapidly diagnose many critical conditions
- Ages 10–20: sequencing the individual with parents and siblings to try to establish the molecular basis for serious, undiagnosed conditions. The genomic information also is useful for disease prevention and sequencing can be done to define a pathogen for more rapid and accurate approaches to infectious diseases.
- After a cancer diagnosis: pinpointing the driver mutations and key biologic underpinning pathways of an individual's cancer
- For treatment of conditions such as diabetes or coronary heart disease: understanding at the individual level which medications might be safer and more effective
- At a sudden death: molecular autopsy via sequencing to determine the cause of death and potentially prevent untimely or avoidable deaths of family members and descendants

---

14   Eric Topol, "Individualized Medicine from Prewomb to Tomb," Cell 157, iss. 1 (March 27, 2014): 241–53, https://dx.doi.org/10.1016/j.cell.2014.02.012.

The Institutional Context

I appreciate the anxiety in government and some medical institutions about people getting results from genome sequencing that they don't understand. We don't want people panicking over test results that suggest they have all sorts of risks that may or may not be real or that they may not be able to control. To the extent that our medical institutions are staffed with genetic specialists, they mostly are in pediatrics, dealing with birth defects. People willing to engage in self-education may get the most benefit now from learning about their genome. In the future, genetic counseling is certainly an area that will grow significantly as more individual genomes get sequenced.

In the meantime, the health tech companies developing AI and algorithms to interpret data from precision medicine will have to guard against potential bias. The problem goes beyond assumptions of biases introduced by geeky young data scientists with limited life experiences writing algorithms. In the future, the machines will write their own algorithms. The scientific establishment has made progress in designing clinical trials to avoid extrapolating conclusions from unrepresentative populations—historically often white males. Machine learning must also be watched for bias from limited sampling. On the upside, if we discover racial, ethnic, or other demographic variations in gene-based risk, we can better target therapies to specific groups of people. Many of these genetic illnesses, such as Tay-Sachs disease and sickle cell anemia, have been studied in detail, but genomic testing may lead to more discoveries or better under-

> **People willing to engage in self-education may get the most benefit now from learning about their genome.**

standing of known variations in incidence rates of common conditions like high blood pressure.

The policymakers who decide what government health programs and private medical insurance will fund should realize that personalized medicine can be an excellent use of resources. If people at risk are identified before they develop illnesses, appropriate intervention is sure to reduce costs. Research has shown that most healthcare costs come in people's final years, and the bulk of the costs are incurred by a small segment of the population. If those older, more chronically ill people had been identified as at-risk two or three decades earlier, interventions in lifestyle or medication or other preventive steps could have prevented them from ending up where they are in our healthcare institutions. New technology will play a part, but we also know that trusted members of a community can be enlisted to improve its health. An interesting study in Texas more than 10 years ago showed improved hypertension control when barbers were trained to perform regular blood pressure checks on African American men in their shops.[15] The idea of such community outreach was built upon elsewhere more recently with successful results.[16] The more that individuals know about their personal vulnerabilities, the more they can participate along with the medical establishment in reducing the risk they will end up in that small segment of the population that consumes the vast majority of healthcare resources.

---

15   National Institutes of Health, "Barbers Help Black Men Beat High Blood Pressures, nih.gov, published March 14, 2011, https://www.nih.gov/news-events/nih-research-matters/barbers-help-black-men-beat-high-blood-pressure.

16   Ronald G. Victor et al., "A Cluster-Randomized Trial of Blood-Pressure Reduction in Black Barbershops," The New England Journal of Medicine 378 (April 5, 2018): 1291–1301, https://doi.org/10.1056/NEJMoa1717250.

Circling Back

Ultimately, investing in wellness and prevention is intimately tied to personalized medicine, bringing us back to the definition of precision medicine as "an emerging approach for disease treatment and prevention that takes into account individual variability in genes, environment, and lifestyle for each person." Measurements that get down to an individual level, whether done in a barber chair, at home, or by a genetic testing company can provide knowledge to make informed decisions about our health. The science is advancing on its own, and it is becoming cheaper and easier to get good data. In the pages ahead we will examine how that data collection has become decentralized, what challenges are resulting for healthcare consumers and providers, and what safeguards can be put in place.

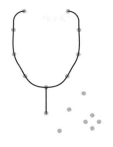

CHAPTER 5

Decentralization Is Driving Changing Circumstances

Near the end of March 2022, Quebec Health Minister Christian Dubé held a news conference to explain a 50-point plan to reform the province's public healthcare system. My phone wouldn't stop ringing that day because one prominent point was to adopt an innovation that I had introduced a year earlier—the command center I alluded to in chapter 3. Within a few days, my colleagues and I at the Jewish General Hospital were explaining to the news media why the health minister was portraying our command center as a template for other regional

Technology that people can use at home without being experts changes our world.

healthcare providers to follow.[17] The government plan acknowledged that the provincial healthcare system was under stress. Almost a million people were on waiting lists to get a family doctor.

As the *Montreal Gazette* put it, the health ministry's plan was "spurred in part both by its successes during the pandemic and its failings, including an acute labour shortage, inadequate care for seniors and outdated data storage and information technologies."[18] In contrast, the computer monitors in our command center gave us complete 24-hour-a-day visibility on patient flow across our 34 sites. We could see where we had service capacity to provide beds, and we could monitor COVID-19 patients in the new hospital-at-home program described in chapter 3. Across the province and in many other places around the world, too many people were coming to hospital emergency rooms as a last resort for care they should have gotten more efficiently in a less costly and more convenient place and time. That care might be in-home or close to home, but more importantly, it would be decentralized from the medical centers that once were the sole repositories of the knowledge and expensive equipment needed for so much diagnosis and treatment.

How Decentralization Evolves

Decentralization doesn't result from a top-down dictate. A governing party may have a 50-point plan, but the elements, like our command

---

17 René Bruemmer, "New Command Centre at Jewish General Speeds Up Patient Flow," Montreal Gazette, April 2, 2022, https://montrealgazette.com/news/local-news/new-command-centre-at-jewish-general-speeds-up-patient-flow#:~:text=The%20system%20is%20designed%20to,Ministry%20as%20one%20to%20emulate.

18 René Bruemmer, "Quebec Health-Care Reform Prioritizes Access to Front-Line Services," Montreal Gazette, March 29, 2022, https://montrealgazette.com/news/local-news/quebec-health-care-reform-prioritizes-access-to-front-line-services.

center, emerge as we adapt to changing needs and technologies. Our rapid assembly of a command center resembled the way Apple put together its teams of young geeks back in the early 1980s when Steve Jobs was working on the original Macintosh computer. Technology that people can use at home without being experts, like the TytoCare Medical Exam Kit mentioned in chapter 3, changes our world. People don't need a doctor to put a medical instrument into their mouth or ears when an affordable gadget can talk them through doing the exam properly themselves at home. Transmitting an image from such a device to the doctor when necessary is not a big technological leap from messaging pictures from a smartphone to loved ones around the globe. Tests once done in clinics and laboratories are happening at a wider variety of points of care—in homes as well as in doctors' offices, urgent care centers, or public health vans.

A digital innovator may launch a product that promises a cheaper, more convenient diagnostic method. If the startup company cannot scale up the product to meet its potential market, there are plenty of large public companies eager to jump in. The prospect of the world's biggest, most technologically advanced corporations like Apple and Amazon taking over healthcare is the paradox of decentralization. What is being decentralized is the sphere of influence of the medical professions' legacy stakeholders. As Dr. Zeev Neuwirth wrote in his 2019 book *Reframing Healthcare*, the medical sector's executives must recognize that transformative change is needed because well-intentioned "improvements" within the current framework will never be enough to resolve systemic problems of access, quality of care, patient safety and trust, and cost.[19] Technology companies are just doing what

---

19 Zeev Neuwirth, Reframing Healthcare: A Roadmap for Creating Disruptive Change (Charleston, SC: Advantage Media Group, 2019).

they do, and government overseers are left trying to figure out how to regulate any of it.

The evolution takes on a life of its own because it empowers people. Once they have seen the convenience of point-of-care testing and home self-examinations, they are not going to want to go back to making appointments and traveling to clinics or laboratories if they don't have to. People like having control over their time and their own bodies, but the tradeoff is they must take more responsibility and be accountable for getting the test or exam done properly. They can't blame the doctor they never saw. And here again, we have a paradox because doctors are worried that they will end up holding the bag one way or another. It remains to be seen how much of this concern is warranted, but doctors worry they may get sicker patients who neglected to use the new technology, were intimidated by it, didn't trust it, or didn't have access. Doctors worry they will take the blame for what they didn't do even though they were not supposed to be doing it anymore. Empowering one part of an ecosystem can disempower or disincentivize another part of the ecosystem as the balance of power and control shifts.

As decentralization empowers people to take care of themselves more, it runs up against the reluctance of some people to accept responsibility for doing so. There always will be people who would rather hand over responsibility to someone else. As an analogy, consider the wide-ranging way able-bodied adults feed themselves. Some go to the grocery store and buy raw ingredients that they whip up into a nutritious

> **Empowering one part of an ecosystem can disempower or disincentivize another part of the ecosystem as the balance of power and control shifts.**

meal—others, not so much. We all enjoy convenience, so given the opportunity we will happily order a gourmet meal cooked by someone else. We approach our healthcare with a somewhat similar consumer mentality.

Systems and Incentives

In North America and many countries around the world, healthcare systems primarily use a fee-for-service model despite its negative impacts on efficiency and affordability. Governments or insurance companies have found it easy and convenient to administer a schedule of fees for doctor or hospital visits and tests, but many studies have proven this system incentivizes wasteful overtreatment. It rewards doctors based on the quantity, not the quality, of the work they perform or the costliness of the services they order because payments are disconnected from outcomes. Efforts by the payers and medical associations to rationalize fee-for-service by determining reasonable costs have failed to alleviate the market distortion. The complexity of medical care is certainly a factor. To compare prices, consumers would have to wade through more than 70,000 diagnostic codes and understand which ones applied to their situation.

Governments can be just as stymied as consumers in trying to rationalize medical expenses. In the United States, the Centers for Medicare & Medicaid Services bases much of its price setting on recommendations from a committee of doctors convened in private by the American Medical Association, which is both a union and a political lobbying group. Specialist physicians have disproportionately more votes on the committee than primary care doctors, and they have no incentive to reduce their pay if technology streamlines a procedure. In Quebec, healthcare is a public system in which the provincial government gives a lump sum of money to the unions representing general practitioners and medical specialists. They each negotiate with the government for their share of the available money. The specialists' bargaining unit is in turn composed of many subspecialty associations that periodically haggle over their piece of the pie. Once each association knows what it has coming, it sets fee schedules based on factors such as the number of members and the types of procedures performed. Not included in the calculations are the quality and appropriateness of care. A subspecialty with numerous providers has more seats at the table and more influence to reward its own work with higher payments. As a surgeon who performed relatively rare operations at a major medical center, it didn't make sense to me that the more numerous general surgeons at community hospitals could win disproportionately high rates for minor procedures like removing hemorrhoids. But they had the power of numbers. Decentralization shifts power back toward the patients by creating more of a free-market, value-based system.

> **Decentralization shifts power back toward the patients by creating more of a free-market, value-based system.**

Influential research led by Professor Michael E. Porter at the Harvard Business School Institute for Strategy & Competitiveness concluded:

> Delivering the right care at the right location in a multi-site care delivery system is a key element of a value-based health care system. To integrate care effectively, providers need to re-define the scope of services at each facility and rationalize the benefit of each site as a component of the whole organization. For instance, high-cost and highly

resourced downtown medical campuses may be better suited for complex medical conditions, while regional care centers may be better suited for lower acuity, more routine, and higher volume services. This strategy will allow concentration of volume by medical condition to fewer locations[20].

In other words, decentralization results in the most difficult procedures being performed in settings like a downtown medical center where they are done at high volume and are more likely to be successful. There always will be a need for world-class hospitals, but more common and less difficult procedures will be performed less expensively somewhere else. The healthcare network I lead has written into our mission statement that we provide "a continuum of healthcare and social services throughout our network of institutions" and "compassionate care and services that are centered on the user and create an exceptional user experience." This healthcare approach should lower costs the same way prices fall when any product or service becomes a commodity. As the individual becomes the center of the medical economy, companies that are used to selling devices and supplies to hospitals and doctors' practices must learn to refocus their marketing on the end consumer. In some cases, they will realize they must rely on retailers, and their medical devices will end up on the shelves of a Walmart or Walgreens.

---

20   "Systems Integration," Harvard Business School Institute for Strategy & Competitiveness, accessed March 6, 2022, https://www.isc.hbs.edu/health-care/value-based-health-care/key-concepts/Pages/systems-integration.aspx.

Care Everywhere

Those invested personally, financially, or emotionally in monolithic healthcare taking place in a large medical center will have to adjust to a changing world. Just as in the pandemic-fueled transition to working more from home and less from offices, there is no going back to the former status quo. The hospital-at-home program we created to avoid our beds being filled with COVID-19 patients has been expanding as I write this. We are monitoring patients at home with congestive heart failure and chronic obstructive lung disease and people recovering from heart attacks. Most people offered the prospect of recovering at home are eager to do so because they are much happier there than in a hospital. This observation was documented at the outset of the program when we asked patients and their families to rate the experience on a scale of 1 to 10. We heard "10" unconditionally, and the respondents all had their own examples of why being at home was better, whether it involved food, work, or family. One woman said that not being away from her three children and knowing she could deal with family issues more directly sped her recovery.

We decided to make the early discharges from the hospital to the hospital-at-home program voluntary and accept anyone back if they changed their minds because they had to have a certain level of family support. Just one of the patients in the initial COVID-19 program came back to the hospital, and it was because family members were uncomfortable with the tech-

> **Most people offered the prospect of recovering at home are eager to do so because they are much happier there than in a hospital.**

nology required for at-home care. The patient would have preferred to stay at home.

We were inventing jobs as we went along in creating the program: working with the patients and families to determine their abilities in home healthcare, educating them about the technology, and training professionals to provide remote care. It was all new, and what we realized was that patients at home were getting more attention than they would have gotten in the hospital. The technology was checking their vital signs more often or more continuously than would happen in a hospital room outside of the intensive care unit. Staffing the command center around the clock with people who could monitor the data was labor intensive, but that cost will decline soon as AI allows the machines to do the work.

The hospital-at-home program is just one example of decentralized "care everywhere." The 50-point reform plan I mentioned proposed a greatly expanded portal service in Quebec in which people can gain access to doctors, nurses, social workers, and mental health professionals by phone or online. It also proposed to have the state system pay for more surgeries in private clinics. Health systems everywhere developed backlogs of surgeries and other medical procedures after they were interrupted by COVID-19. Burnout from dealing with the pandemic also worsened an existing shortage of healthcare providers, a problem the US government committed $100 million to address in October 2021. Funding and budgets must be adjusted to the new realities in healthcare, especially where funding is based on how many hospital beds are full. Medical education, hiring, training, and licensing all need to adjust as well.

PANDEMIC DISRUPTION

The COVID-19 pandemic forced people to have remote visits with their doctors, and policymakers had to rapidly adjust to a new reality, lifting regulations and increasing payments for telehealth. Virtual care went from being a niche disrupter to being widely known and accepted, though still in a building stage. KPMG International surveyed 200 healthcare CEOs in the US, Canada, and six other countries in 2021. Reporting the results in November of that year, Dr. Anna van Poucke said more than 6 in 10 were fundamentally revising approaches in four areas: workforce, digital delivery models, business operations, and care-delivery models. Of the majority of CEOs who said they had transformations underway prepandemic, 97 percent said COVID-19 "significantly accelerated" their transformation efforts. The KPMG presentation called this "the COVID cloud's silver lining."[21]

How Fast Will It Happen?

Several years ago, I might have believed that some of this decentralization, like the hospital-at-home program, would be stalled by an ivory-tower mindset common among specialist physicians. These doctors would feel it was their decision when a patient was ready to be discharged. And they would have insisted on being present for some treatments, visits, and follow-ups now handled by allied healthcare professionals. That resistance is crumbling, and decentralization is

---

21 Anna van Poucke, "Healthcare CEO Future Pulse 2021," (presentation, KPMG International, November 11, 2021).

popular among the physiotherapists, occupational therapists, pharmacists, social workers, and other health professionals who are practicing at the top of their license. One hesitation I have seen is that physicians don't want to find themselves running back and forth between the virtual hospital and the brick-and-mortar hospital. They don't mind training for a new job in virtual medicine or changing jobs, but they don't want to be doing a second job on top of the current one.

With any change, some people will want to move faster than others. Some leaders will try to speed a transformation by starting with changing their organizational culture. I disagree with that approach. In setting up our command center and hospital-at-home program, I didn't try to change the company culture. I just turned to two creative thinkers on the executive staff who I knew would be thrilled to be empowered to do something outside their job description. I gave them carte blanche to pull in whoever they needed who was willing to help without worrying about costs or the hierarchy of reporting in the organization. Our chief digital health officer and one of his key team members worked nonstop for 72 hours to make sure the technological infrastructure was stood up. It was a real-life example of something we discussed on a theoretical level in chapter 2, how changes emerge in complex adaptive systems. No doubt though, changes to organizational culture will follow as part of a focus on adaptive change leadership.

POTENTIAL COST SAVINGS

A 2019 article in the *Journal of the American Medical Association* offered a succinct summary of the causes and extent of waste in the US healthcare system and considered the potential for savings.

The authors focused on six known areas of waste: failure of care delivery, failure of care coordination, overtreatment or low-value care, pricing failure, fraud and abuse, and administrative complexity. Using dozens of prior studies and reports, the researchers estimated a range of total annual cost in each area of waste. It added up to $760 billion to $935 billion a year, accounting for about 25 percent of total healthcare spending. They estimated annual savings from measures to eliminate waste in five of the six areas, since they found no studies on interventions targeting administrative complexity. The range of potential savings was $191 billion to $286 billion, which the authors said represents a potential 25 percent reduction in the total cost of waste.[22]

Circling Back

Grabbing people from different departments on the fly to set up a command center and respond to the needs of patients during the COVID-19 wave was a manifestation of decentralization. The organizational governance structure follows the invention of the product. Form follows function. Ideally, the technology that allows us to provide the right care in the right place at the right time should produce efficiency and cost savings.

Our institutional, legal, economic, and regulatory structures must adapt to the emergent decentralization. In a decentralized healthcare

---

22   William H. Shrank, Teresa L. Rogstad, Natasha Parekh, "Waste in the US Health Care System: Estimated Costs and Potential for Savings," Journal of the American Medical Association 322, no. 15 (October 15, 2019): 1501–9, https://doi.org/10.1001/jama.2019.13978.

system, we are more interested in outcomes and results than in structures. As the individual becomes the center of the medical economy, companies that are used to selling devices and supplies to hospitals and doctors' practices must learn to refocus their marketing on the end consumer. Healthcare institutions also must learn to focus on what other industries call the customer experience. Centering healthcare on people is empowering to individuals and will lead to better outcomes and more sustainable systems. Many physicians are reluctant to give up the control they have in managing their patients' healthcare, but the pages ahead will explain why that has already begun happening. Technology is fueling amazing but sometimes chaotic changes in access to health information and knowledge.

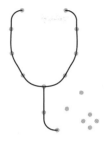

C H A P T E R   6

Democratization of Knowledge

In a shadowy marketplace on the internet, scammers buy stolen data from hackers using what's called dark web encryption technology to stay anonymous. We have known for many years that medical records are a "hot commodity" on the dark web, as the American business magazine *Fast Company* described it in a 2016 story.[23] Hackers can sell medical records for much higher prices than some other data used in identity thefts, such as bank or credit card information, for several reasons. The healthcare records usually connect an individual to a much wider array of sensitive information, including birth dates, phone numbers, Social Security numbers, diagnoses, and medical test results. This information cannot be easily replaced, like getting a new

---

23   Christina Farr, "On the Dark Web Medical Records Are a Hot Commodity,"
     Fast Company, July 7, 2016, https://www.fastcompany.com/3061543/
     on-the-dark-web-medical-records-are-a-hot-commodity.

credit card number. Criminals can use healthcare data for identity theft, blackmail, extortion, and—most profitably—insurance fraud. The *AARP Bulletin*, a magazine widely read by older Americans, called theft from government healthcare programs "arguably the costliest fraud in America."[24] The April 2022 report said an estimated 5 to 10 percent of the US Medicare budget is lost to fraudulent billing.

Researchers using US government data published a study in 2019 intended to show how widespread health records breaches had become.[25] From October 2009 through June 2017, they estimated the breaches affected at least 173 million people, more than half the American population. Interestingly, the researchers were from Canada, Poland, and Russia, and they published their findings in an Iranian journal. They were issuing a transnational warning message that more resources and attention are needed in Iran and everywhere to protect private health information. The fact that the breaches were tallied in the US reflected the fact that Americans have privacy laws requiring public notifications that enabled the researchers to download real-time data from an official website on the extent of the breaches. But it's not a first-world problem. In 2020, security researchers found more than 230,000 Indonesian COVID-19 patients' records on the dark web.[26] And if vital medical information is corrupted or lost during hacking, people's health and lives could be at stake. In ransomware attacks, the criminals encrypt medical center computers to hold the stored data hostage. Doctors and patients eager to get on with treatments and surgeries may pressure the administrators to pay the ransom.

---

24   Joe Eaton, "The Medicare Scammers," AARP Bulletin, April 2022, 22–3.

25   Waldemar W. Koczkodaj et al., "Massive Health Record Breaches Evidenced by the Office for Civil Rights Data," Iranian Journal of Public Health 48, no. 2 (February 2019): 278–88, https://www.ncbi.nlm.nih.gov/pmc/articles/PMC6556182.

26   "Over 230K Indonesian COVID-19 Patients' Records Exposed on Darknet," CISO MAG, June 24, 2020, https://cisomag.com/indonesian-patients-data-leak/.

This criminality is an unintended consequence of the information being available and not properly protected. It's a huge problem, but only one of the barriers that stand between our ability to produce information and cultivate a more effective democratization of knowledge. In this context, it may be helpful to think of information as anything you might be able to read somewhere, and then think of knowledge as something you acquire when you understand what you're reading. The democratization of medical knowledge began as the internet and other technologies dispersed it from the brains of specialist physicians to a broader number of allied healthcare professionals and from large medical centers out into communities.

Access, Consent, and Privacy

People have amazing access to health information these days, often to the consternation of doctors, who feel they are wasting valuable time dealing with unnecessary questions and unwarranted anxieties that patients bring them after searching symptoms online. This access is the inevitable result of the trends we have been discussing—the emerging complexity of networks and systems, digitalization, and real-time and connected healthcare. This access can empower people to take more control over their health, but we have many issues to address on the way to that goal. Our societies are just beginning to grapple with who has access to whose information and under what conditions. The widespread criminality on the dark web shows that

> The widespread criminality on the dark web shows that we are in a Wild West phase of what should be the development of rational and effective controls over consent and privacy.

we are in a Wild West phase of what should be the development of rational and effective controls over consent and privacy.

Technological advances will soon resolve some of the issues. Those people searching their symptoms online will be better informed because algorithms will improve as AI gets better at rooting out misinformation. AI also will help triage the information available to healthcare providers and regulators, and we will develop better security against data breaches. Of course, technological advances also are available to those scammers on the dark web and to small entrepreneurs and giant corporations that find ways to profit from buying and selling our health data.

Governments around the world are at various stages of regulating digital privacy in general and more specifically health information. The European Union adopted a General Data Protection Regulation (GDPR) in 2016 and made it effective in 2018. That year, the Canadian government began developing a Digital Charter intended to allow companies to make productive use of data without violating people's trust.[27] Canada's Digital Charter was partly modeled after the California Consumer Privacy Act, one of the first laws giving people rights to the data companies collect from them. These laws are notoriously unwieldy to implement, as they have high compliance costs for businesses while providing limited benefits to consumers. A business might have to tell you the type but not the name of third parties it shares your personal information with, and then only if you know how to ask for the information. You may have the right to ask a company to delete your personal information, but first you must fill out a form proving your identity by disclosing personal information.

---

27   Government of Canada, "Canada's Digital Charter: Trust in a digital world," canada.ca, accessed January 3, 2023, https://ised-isde.canada.ca/site/innovation-better-canada/en/canadas-digital-charter-trust-digital-world.

The Canadian government offered this rationale for the Digital Charter Implementation Act, 2020:[28]

Meaningful consent: Modernized consent rules would ensure that individuals have the plain-language information they need to make meaningful choices about the use of their personal information.

Data mobility: To further improve their control, individuals would have the right to direct the transfer of their personal information from one organization to another. For example, individuals could direct their bank to share their personal information with another financial institution.

Disposal of personal information and withdrawal of consent: The accessibility of information online makes it hard for individuals to control their online identity. The legislation would allow individuals to request that organizations dispose of personal information and, in most cases, permit individuals to withdraw consent for the use of their information.

Algorithmic transparency: The Consumer Privacy Protection Act contains new transparency requirements that apply to automated decision-making systems like algorithms and artificial intelligence. Businesses would have to be transparent about how they use such systems to make significant predictions, recommendations, or decisions about individuals. Individuals would also have the right to request that businesses explain how a prediction,

---

28 Government of Canada, "Fact Sheet: Digital Charter Implementation Act, 2020," canada.ca, accessed December 15, 2022, https://ised-isde.canada.ca/site/innovation-better-canada/en/canadas-digital-charter/strengthening-privacy-digital-age/fact-sheet-digital-charter-implementation-act-2020.

recommendation, or decision was made by an automated decision-making system and explain how the information was obtained.

Deidentified information: The practice of removing direct identifiers (such as a name) from personal information is becoming increasingly common, but the rules that govern how this information is then used are not clear. The legislation will clarify that this information must be protected and that it can be used without an individual's consent only under certain circumstances.

Though imperfect, data privacy regulation is a necessary step toward people's empowerment to control their own health. When they seek healthcare, they should know who owns the information that they give about their family history and that is generated from their appointments, examinations, tests, and diagnoses. Is the information the property of the healthcare organization or the physician? Is it being held securely from dark web scammers? Can someone in the data chain of custody share it with life sciences companies, such as Big Pharma? Or does the patient own the information?

Empowering the Individual

Ideally, when we are teaching our children reading, writing, and arithmetic, they also will be learning how to take control of their wellness and healthcare. This teaching should go far beyond the brief lessons we got in grade school that fruits and vegetables are good for us—the basics of diet and how our bodies work. Once children get into high school, they already may have developed bad health habits, including smoking and drug abuse, so it's too late to teach them to turn the amazing health information out there for them into action-able knowledge.

We all have heard or read stories about patients coming up with their own diagnosis that was both correct and a total surprise to their doctor. Those stories are increasingly common with the democra-tization of healthcare knowledge, which has greatly changed how we approach the practice of medicine and train physicians. When I went through medical school, doctors were at the pinnacle of health-care, handing down commandments like Moses coming down from Mount Sinai. Now healthcare delivery is more team based. Allied healthcare professionals are better and more broadly trained than ever, allowing them to practice at the top of their license and have access to knowledge previously limited to specialist physicians. Physicians who treat someone for an acute episode have a professional colleague to hand that person off to for managing the more mundane issues that most doctors never dealt with.

At the same time, more people feel empowered with information that's available to them to become equal partners in their healthcare. In this context, the word "patient," which we use for lack of a better term, seems to wrongly connote that someone is suffering from some condition and passively awaiting help from medical experts. I have repeatedly referred to "the individ-ual," but that's not always the right word either. Each of us is in charge

> **Each of us is in charge of our own system of personal-ized healthcare.**

of our own system of personalized healthcare. We decide where to go for help, not always starting with a doctor. Communities of kindred souls have come together to support each other with specific health-care challenges. These communities can be extremely valuable, especially to people dealing with cancer, diabetes, Alzheimer's disease, or other serious and chronic physical or mental health conditions in themselves or their family members. These communities can help inform people about clinical trials of new therapies and warn people when treatments that are marginally useful to a small number of patients are being marketed as more widely effective than they really are. With the help of social media, these communities exist on a scale that would have been impossible before the internet. That's another aspect of the democratization of knowledge.

The Value of Your Data

In chapter 4 we discussed how the health tech company 23andMe marketed a direct-to-consumer genetic test. In the ensuing years, 23andMe sold its data to pharmaceutical companies to use in developing drugs. In 2018, GlaxoSmithKline gained exclusive rights to use 23andMe data for drug development, and it purchased a $300 million stake in the company. Less than two years later, 23andMe licensed a drug it had developed itself.[29] The company is proud that its data is being used to better understand the genetic aspects of disease and develop treatments. It is questionable, though, whether the millions of people who provided saliva samples to learn about their ancestry realized they were contributing to commercial drug projects. Those who opted in to share their genetic data for research did so in a wholesale way, as we all do when we click "accept" on the legal policy pages of so many social media and consumer websites. The genetic test takers were not able to know which companies would use their data, or how, or why.

---

29   Megan Molteni, "23andMe's Pharma Deals Have Been the Plan All Along," Wired, August 3, 2018, https://www.wired.com/story/23andme-glaxosmithkline-pharma-deal.

If I own my genetic data as an individual citizen, should the drug companies be coming to me to sign an acquisition contract for my personal medical information? That generally doesn't happen now. A hospital or other healthcare provider usually signs the research agreement on behalf of its patients, who may or may not be asked for their consent. Practices vary by jurisdiction. In Quebec, a bill was introduced that basically makes the provincial government the owner of personal medical information, and it remains to be seen how the government will use that power. The stated goal is to promote efficient information sharing between patients, their caregivers, managers, and researchers, something that was found lacking during the initial response to COVID-19. The health minister said one aim of the new law was to promote developing innovative treatments but that this would occur without commercial sale of personal data.[30] This bill died on the order paper before it could be adopted because of a pending election. However the governing party was re-elected in October 2022 and the proposed legislation, Bill 3, was reintroduced with modifications that should let patients more easily consult their health file, know who had access to their information and decide if they want to share that information with other professionals.[31]

Still, it remains to be seen whether the bill could represent an infringement on personal privacy rights. I think the role of the government is to do exactly as Canada's Digital Charter suggests, making sure appropriate provisions and protections are in place to protect patients and their data.

---

30   The Canadian Press, "Quebec Tables Bills to Make Sharing Health Information More Efficient," CTV News Montreal, December 3, 2021, https://montreal.ctvnews. ca/quebec-tables-bills-to-make-sharing-health-information-more-efficient-1.5692812.

31   Ugo Giguère, "New Quebec Bill Seeks to Modernize Patients' Access to Health Data," Montreal Gazette, December 7, 2022, https://montrealgazette.com/news/ quebec/new-quebec-bill-seeks-to-modernize-patients-access-to-health-data.

The drafters of that bill recognized that simply removing people's names and other directly identifying information is not enough to protect their privacy. Researchers designing our next-generation drugs want individual-level data that includes demographics, full medical histories, laboratory test results, and so much other information that it really isn't anonymous. They want to dig into the molecular biology of what's going on in each patient. A privacy workaround on the horizon known as synthetic data artificially recreates the statistical characteristics of real patients so the data can be used without going through the traditional ethics consent process.

WHAT IS SYNTHETIC DATA?

Here's how the website of a small Israeli company called MDClone described it: synthetic data is nonreversible, artificially created data that replicates the statistical characteristics and correlations of real-world, raw data. Utilizing both discrete and nondiscrete variables of interest, synthetic data does not contain identifiable information because it uses a statistical approach to create a brand new data set. While it's possible to identify an individual with anonymized data or deidentified data by inferring characteristics, cross-referencing data similarities, or reversing the data approach, MDClone's synthetic data is the only anonymization method that fully prevents reidentification.[32]

Healthcare providers traditionally treat the patient as a consumer, but how does that notion apply when there's a financial transaction in which they are selling the individual's information? At

---

32   MDClone, "What Is Synthetic Data?," MDClone, accessed December 12, 2022,
       https://www.mdclone.com/synthetic-data.

that point, maybe the researchers or pharmaceutical companies are the consumers because it's the patient who has something of value to sell.

Circling Back

Empowering individuals with not only information but also understanding and knowledge of how to take control of their health is a positive development, but it carries a lot of complications. Decisions must be made about who has access to our private health information, who owns it, and under what conditions it can be sold or transferred to third parties. Given the sensitivity and value of health data, institutions are belatedly recognizing their obligation to protect our privacy from theft and misuse. As health information in general becomes more widely available, doctors have had to adjust to having others encroaching on their realm of expertise. More people have the knowledge to take more responsibility for the wellness of themselves or others in their care. In the process, they must learn proper use of the technology that has helped give them their newfound knowledge, as we will discuss in the next chapter.

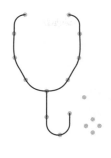

CHAPTER 7

Democratization
of Technology

An ultrasound machine used to be a big deal in terms of size, so they were mostly confined to the radiology departments of hospitals. The machines eventually were portable enough to be wheeled to the side of a patient's stretcher bed, where a radiologist or special technician would perform the ultrasound. Ultrasound migrated into other specialties over the years. Cardiologists began using ultrasound to evaluate how heart valves are functioning. Obstetricians or their nurses used them for predelivery checkups of pregnant women. Today, handheld ultra-sounds could fit in a large pocket or small purse. Emergency room physicians perform abdominal and chest ultrasounds as a screening procedure to determine which patients need a trip to the radiology department. Nurses use them every day to identify blood vessels where they can stick large-bore intravenous catheters.

This miniaturization of technology is familiar in that we have seen it play out in many devices in our homes and workplaces. Our children live in an entirely different world than the one we grew up in as technological development has accelerated with the exponential growth of computing power. What will healthcare look like when those children are adults or seniors? Dr. Bertalan Meskó, director of the Medical Futurist Institute, has sketched a picture for us. In his 2022 article "Looking Back at Today's Healthcare in 2060," he described "a utopian future of healthcare" through an imagined conversation with his granddaughter, Nina. They have what Meskó calls CubeSensors throughout their home, designed to "measure air quality, temperature, humidity, noise, light, air pressure" and optimize factors as needed based on their personal information. Nina has grown up with CubeSensors all her life; she tells Meskó that she hasn't even heard the word "hospital," much less been seen by a human doctor. Gone are the days of paper records and universal rather than personalized medicine doses. We once struggled to correct malfunctioning organs; now, Meskó tells Nina, we never again have to worry about finding a viable donor. AI allows us to print tissues designed specifically for each patient. Robots perform surgery, and blindness is reversible. Cancer is treatable, and not at a high cost. As her grandfather revels in just how far we've come, Nina drifts off to

> **The democratization of technology is not just driven by advances in the design of medical devices but more by who is using them and how they are doing so.**

sleep, oblivious to the barbaric practices of the past that her grandfather lived through.[33]

Meskó depicts a future in which patients are "equal partners of physicians," care is both affordable and preventable, and information is accessible and digital. I share his optimism based on what I see happening around me in my hospital and health network, including the miniaturization, mobility, decreased cost, and ease of use that make ultrasound technology more available and usable by healthcare providers not previously qualified or able to use it. This is an example of the democratization of technology being a consequence of the democratization of knowledge and vice versa. Each allows the other to happen because the democratization of technology is not just driven by advances in the design of medical devices but more by who is using them and how they are doing so.

An Asynchronous Movement

Some medical practices are more likely than others to move in the direction where AI performs diagnoses previously done by specialist physicians. Nurses can staff online visits in which AI can evaluate a skin lesion and make a diagnosis as good or better than dermatologists can. Radiology is rapidly moving in the same direction. Other examples are the remote monitoring of wearable sensors that we described in chapter 3 and the genetic testing we discussed in chapter 4. Anything a software company can create that provides a medical benefit could qualify as a digital therapeutic device. Some devices require remote monitoring, as we are doing in the command center of our hospital-at-home program, but there are others that people can use on their own. Consider the potential efficiencies: if one product

---

33   Bertalan Meskó, "Looking Back at Today's Healthcare in 2060," The Medical
      Futurist, April 26, 2022, https://medicalfuturist.com/healthcare-in-2060.

can educate many patients to better manage chronic diseases and look out for their own wellness, society will spend less on healthcare, and doctor and nurse shortages will be alleviated.

Despite medical devices being heavily regulated and requiring time-consuming research and testing, billions of dollars have flowed into this consumer-product market. Elon Musk, the entrepreneur behind Tesla and SpaceX, started a brain-implant company called Neuralink. It's not the only company working on brain-machine interfaces, which could help people who are paralyzed or who have lost the ability to speak. Implanting electrodes into people's skulls to give them more control over their bodies is just an extreme example of where the tech companies are headed. On the fast track are smart-phone apps that give people actionable data on common diseases such as diabetes.

This democratization of technology carries an obligation to update our systems for training and accountability to ensure the technology is being used correctly, and the devices are properly certified for what they are being used for. You may have a good example right in front of you of a pretty good medical device that has not been certified for at least some of its uses. Mobile phones and smart watches have health-related features but are not marketed as medical devices, so they do not need to have government regulatory approval for diagnostic or therapeutic uses. The latest Apple Watch, as I write this, can measure oxygen saturation in the blood, which became widely known as an important health indicator during the first COVID-19 wave. But Apple issued a prominent disclaimer: "Measurements taken with the Blood Oxygen app are not intended for medical use and are only designed for general fitness and wellness purposes." I don't know how useful it is for me to monitor my blood oxygen during exercise, but it is useful data in a medical setting. Devices such as the Apple Watch also can take an electrocardiogram and monitor for irregular heartbeats, such as atrial fibrillation.[34]. I have no doubt those apps have saved people's lives by motivating them to get timely healthcare even when the tech companies have deliberately put off going through the onerous and time-consuming bureaucratic process of getting regulators to certify the devices for medical use. Such business considerations have slowed some advances, but devices that are medical grade and still cheap and simple enough for home use will become more prevalent.

There are several reasons why we should not expect technology to advance uniformly across the healthcare landscape. Large corporations, including pharmacy chains, big-box retailers, and technology providers, are driving the spread of digital therapeutics, such as the devices we can wear or use at home. Direct-to-consumer healthcare appeals to investors and to people who find it more convenient. If you are old enough to remember shaking a glass thermometer to get the mercury level down, you no doubt appreciate the latest labor-saving digital thermometers. For a country like the United States, with an aging population and ever-increasing spending on chronic diseases, consumerization of healthcare is the best hope for dealing with rising medical costs and service shortages, such as the lack of primary-care doctors in many areas. Traditional healthcare providers have lagged in digitalizing some of their functions that people interact with to shop for services, coordinate their care, and understand their benefits. Typically, information technology resources were dedicated first and foremost to business processes, such as billing. Several years ago, the McKinsey Global Institute reported there was a large and growing gap in how much digitalization had occurred in different industry

---

34   Dhruv R. Seshadri et al., "Accuracy of Apple Watch for Detection of Atrial Fibrillation," Circulation (Feb. 24, 2020) https://www.ahajournals.org/doi/10.1161/CIRCULATIONAHA.119.044126.

sectors, and healthcare was near the bottom. "Many health care organizations, for instance, use incredibly sophisticated technology in diagnostics and treatment, but substantial parts of their workforce use only rudimentary or no technology," McKinsey researchers wrote in the Harvard Business Review in 2016.[35]

ELECTRONIC HEALTHCARE RECORDS

Medical-center leaders, including my predecessor CEOs at Montreal's Jewish General Hospital, have often been able to point to a building or an additional pavilion as a visible legacy of the growth and change they helped produce. I had a different legacy in mind as I accepted reappointment to another four-year term in 2022 at an age when some executives already have retired. We had begun codeveloping a next-generation electronic healthcare record, and the additional years would give me a chance to see that product through to implementation. I think it will put the organization in a good position as digital storehouses of medical information become a priority as opposed to building more concrete structures. This priority reflects our network's branding (Care Everywhere) and the wider medical industry embracing the concept of "healthcare without an address." Just as important, studies have found that the current electronic healthcare records systems cause physicians significant stress and burnout by forcing them to do a lot of

---

35 Prashant Gandhi, Somesh Khanna, and Sree Ramaswamy, "Which Industries Are the Most Digital (and Why?)," Harvard Business Review, April 1, 2016, https://hbr.org/2016/04/a-chart-that-shows-which-industries-are-the-most-digital-and-why#:~:text=The%20technology%20sector%20comes%20out,the%20rest%20of%20the%20economy.

time-consuming data entry.[36] They are staring at screens instead of interacting with patients and colleagues, using systems not well-designed to improve clinical care.

Being Equipped for Empowerment

The proliferation of easy-to-use, real-time monitoring provides more data than we've ever had. It is up to us as individuals to turn that data into information that in turn leads to knowledge of how to fit the devices into our regimen of self-care. The data must be captured and displayed to someone who knows what it means, which can involve training the end user, transmitting data to caregivers, and using AI to generate alerts. Those challenges must be overcome to actualize the connected and real-time healthcare we discussed in chapter 3. Before we send anyone out of our hospital to self-monitor at home, we walk them and their family through the process. They may have an app or video to refer to as well, but face-to-face interaction comes first.

Healthcare equity must be an overriding consideration in setting up and administering programs that encourage self-care. Not everyone is technology savvy, not everyone has the necessary language skills to

> **Healthcare equity must be an overriding consideration in setting up and administering programs that encourage self-care.**

---

36   Roger Collier, "Electronic Health Records Contributing to Physician Burnout," Canadian Medical Association Journal 189, no. 45 (November 13, 2017): E1405–6, https://doi.org/10.1503%2Fcmaj.109-5522.

understand, not everyone has the economic wherewithal to afford things such as smart devices, and not everyone has a family member to rely on when needed. Our immigrant patients in Montreal speak 82 languages. Fortunately, there is almost always a relative on hand to interpret the instructions from English or French, but we must reckon with whatever circumstances the individual presents. Some people have been harmed by poor living conditions or other disparities that affect their health, and they may need more access or assistance than better-off patients require. Some examples of healthcare equity initiatives are sending a mobile clinic to an underserved area, using social workers to counsel people on prevention of chronic diseases, and engaging with a community in a culturally sensitive way using understandable language.

People may underestimate the amount of diagnostic equipment they already have and know how to use. Digital thermometers, especially since COVID-19 came upon us, are in a lot of homes, as are COVID test kits. Digital blood-pressure cuffs are increasingly common. Life sciences companies are developing more sophisticated ways to know when people are failing to take their medicine—so that software or even the pill itself can monitor adherence. Even using a bathroom scale every day can be a lifesaver for cardiac patients because someone developing congestive heart failure will retain water and get heavier as a warning sign. These common devices are in addition to ones developed for specific diseases, such as diabetic glucose monitoring and insulin pumps, cardiac pacemakers, and digital infusion devices for cancer chemotherapy. Smart digital devices can transmit signals back to a hospital command center to be read and recorded by machines.

Healthcare is catching up with so many other aspects of our lives in which technology has enabled us to get instant information and feel knowledgeable enough to make our own decisions—about purchases, travel bookings, and investments. Why should the information contained in your body be the exclusive purview of some third-party healthcare provider—like if you had to make an appointment to ask your banker how much money you have? In the past, people wasted a lot of their own time and healthcare system resources visiting an emergency room, clinic, or doctor to have a concern checked out, often needlessly. Now they can do some of the screening at home by themselves or using a telehealthcare provider. They have access not just to what they find in online searches about their symptoms but to their own electronic medical records and personal real-time information they can generate with self-diagnostic equipment simple enough to use effectively.

The stethoscope, which has been around for two centuries, is a good example of the pace at which digitalization affects the democratization of both technology and knowledge. In some places, doctors still listen to people's heart or lungs with an acoustic stethoscope and make their own interpretation of what they are hearing. Newer digital stethoscopes can amplify, filter, record, interpret, store, and transmit sounds, so there should be no mistaking what the sound was and what it means. As with the newer, smaller ultrasound devices, digital stethoscopes can be used by more people in more places. Of course, training is required, and more experienced specialists with more sophisticated equipment should be involved when the users are not sure what they are observing.

MY *TOP GUN* DIGITAL THERAPEUTIC

Some years ago, the US Air Force made a serendipitous medical discovery by observing what happens when fighter pilots are under tremendous G-force pressure. They have a habit of gripping the arms of their airplane cockpit seats, and real-time digital monitoring of vital signs showed their blood pressure fell. Researchers created a device that simulated the gripping part to see if it would lower blood pressure on its own. At the time, my blood pressure was on the high end of normal and I wanted to get it down, so I signed up for a trial of the handgrip device. Studies have found the therapy has some effectiveness.[37]

Keep An Eye on AI

I have been urging my senior management team and their direct reports to educate themselves about artificial intelligence and its applications in their areas of responsibility with the help of research reports we receive from the Advisory Board member network. Deciding how and where to use digital tools is not just the province of the IT department. AI potentially can solve complex problems faster and better than humans, whether we are talking about scheduling hospital facilities, catching billing mistakes, or diagnosing cancers. But it is up to us humans to determine whether the machines are up to a particular task because a lot of our decision-making involves judgment and

---

37 P.J. Millar et al., "Isometric Handgrip Training Lowers Blood Pressure and Increases Heart Rate Complexity in Medicated Hypertensive Patients," Scandinavian Journal of Medicine & Science in Sports 23, no. 5 (January 20, 2012):620–26, https://doi.org/10.1111/j.1600-0838.2011.01435.x.

intuition, and medical diagnosis is an art as much as a science. Not only do humans bring empathy and compassion to the interaction but we also make observations a machine might miss, and we apply common sense.

A 2018 report from the Advisory Board International Global eHealth Executive Council ran through all the cost-saving and time-saving benefits of AI in healthcare but cautioned about "AI's 'black box problem,' which states that increasingly smarter algorithms cannot investigate cause."[38] For example, a recent study found AI was able to identify the race of a person from medical imaging data that contain no indications of race detectable by human experts.[39] Whether that perplexing AI capability is good or bad depends on how it is used. What is clear is that healthcare institutions must be proactive, strategic, and deliberative in adopting AI, asking vendors a lot of questions. Healthcare administrators and policymakers must ensure AI implementation fits their goals and culture and meets the needs of staff and patients.

A Lesson from the Past

In the early to mid-1990s, we had a medical breakthrough called laparoscopic surgery, enabling us to do procedures in a minimally invasive way that formerly involved a lot of cutting people open. Some of us surgeons were excited to be retrained on the new instrumentation, while others, who have thankfully mostly left us, resisted giving up what they knew. The new method inevitably would win out because

---

38 Advisory Board: International Global eHealth Executive Council, "The Artificial Intelligence Ecosystem: Market Trends, Applications, and Considerations for the Future," advisory.com, 2018, 8-17.

39 Judy Wawira Gichoya et al., "AI Recognition of Patient Race in Medical Imaging: A Modelling Study," Lancet Digital Health 4, no. 6 (May 11, 2022): E406–14, https://doi.org/10.1016/S2589-7500(22)00063-2.

patients would rather have surgery through a little keyhole, not a 12-inch incision. Training courses sprang up, some university-based, others sponsored by private companies, but laparoscopic surgery had not yet become mainstream enough to be part of formal certification in general surgery or other surgical specialties. Surgeons would simply see one, do one, and then teach one, as we like to say. As laparoscopic surgery took hold in removal of gallbladders for people who had gallstones, some improperly trained surgeons injured the common bile duct. This part of the gastrointestinal tract that runs between the liver and the upper portion of the small intestine, the duodenum, allows bile to flow out of the liver into the intestine. Malpractice lawsuits began piling up.

Around the same time, my publicly funded hospital had a budget deficit, and my predecessor CEO set out to prove we were not overspending so much as we were underfunded. Government auditors were invited in to look at the books. As chief of surgery, I was asked to attend one of the meetings in the boardroom with the CEO and the auditors.

"It seems to us that your cost of doing surgery is significantly more than what we've seen in other institutions," an auditor said. And I replied, "Can you be more specific?" Once they mentioned some surgical procedures, I asked what other institutions they had been in to audit. As soon as they told me, I knew the reason for the large difference in expenses. At the time, we were one of the few university hospitals in the province doing an increasing amount of minimally invasive surgery, so gallbladder surgery could cost several hundreds of dollars more. But I explained, "It's not the same operation."

"What do you mean?" the auditor asked. "You're both taking out the same gallbladder." And I said, "Yes, but our patients are going home the same day and their patients are staying in the hospital for five to seven days. We have a complication rate close to zero, significantly lower than the rate in the more traditional open procedure. We have no use of blood products. They have a certain percentage use of blood products." Then I asked, "If you came into my hospital today and needed an operation, would you want me to cut you open with a 12-inch incision? Or would you like this keyhole surgery where you can go home a few hours later?"

That explanation satisfied the auditor. But the point of the story is that an advance in technology that empowers a patient brings a lot of obligations throughout a healthcare system, as training, funding, and standard practices must be adjusted to new ways of doing things. People must learn to use the technology so that it works the way it should work, and the people paying the bills need to understand that the game has changed. Now, with the introduction of virtual care and hospital-at-home programs, the game is changing again.

Circling Back

Smaller, cheaper, mobile, easier-to-use diagnostic and therapeutic equipment is filling a niche in healthcare and contributing to its dispersal from large hospitals into community clinics and homes. That decentralization empowers individuals by giving them information they can act on to take control of their own health and wellness. The democratization of technology involves putting tools into the hands of more people to do more to stay informed and gain understanding and control of their health. The result is a loss or shifting of control, which we will explore in the next chapter.

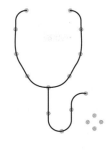

CHAPTER 8

The Devolution of Control

Stop me if you have heard this one: a man goes to his doctor, who says, "I have good news and bad news for you ..." No doubt you have heard one of the dozens of old jokes that start similarly, but in this chapter, we have good news and bad news for the doctor. As allied healthcare professionals have become more competent to perform more of the work previously reserved for physicians, the good news for the doctor is a reduced workload, wasting less time on patients or problems that do not require someone with advanced medical training. The bad news is that to the extent their compensation is based on the number of patients they see, procedures they perform, or other measures of the quantity of care, doctors' income may take a hit. Doctors and their professional associations have been in the paradoxical position of arguing for the good news and against the bad news portion of this zero-sum situation. But it's clear that doctors are experiencing a devolution of control, or to put it metaphorically, they are slipping from the top of the food chain.

In Canada, we are used to physicians being independent agents, but in other jurisdictions, many or most doctors are employed by the government or private corporations. From a business standpoint, it makes sense that whoever is responsible for the budget of a hospital or healthcare network should have control over physicians because they are the primary driver of the institutions' costs. Fewer doctors than ever work for themselves in the United States. The American Medical Association reported in 2021 that a majority of US patient-care physicians work outside of private practice. The AMA found an accelerating shift in practice size and ownership because of mergers and acquisitions, private-practice closures, physician job changes, and younger doctors taking a different path than those retiring.[40] The trends we have been discussing throughout this book also have the inevitable consequence of more physicians working as hospital employees. The more routine work that has been performed in private practices not only can be handled by allied healthcare professionals but soon by machines or people using emerging technology in their homes. This reality led CVS Health in September 2022 to initiate an $8 billion acquisition of Signify Health and obtain the technology that supports that company's network of doctors making house calls. Amazon also appears to be relying on acquisitions to buy its way into the healthcare market.[41] In July 2022, Amazon made a $3.9 billion acquisition of

---

40 American Medical Association, "AMA Analysis Shows Most Physicians Work Outside of Private Practice," press release, May 5, 2021, https://www.ama-assn.org/press-center/press-releases/ama-analysis-shows-most-physicians-work-outside-private-practice.

41 Caroline O'Donovan, "Amazon Care Is Dead, but the Tech Giant's Health-Care Ambitions Live On," Washington Post, September 4, 2022, https://www.washingtonpost.com/technology/2022/09/04/amazon-care-health-one-medical.

One Medical, offering a premium price for a not-yet-profitable primary-care provider. One Medical had 188 offices in 25 US markets, but its draw was that patients paid an annual fee for a technology-powered experience, such as on-demand video consultations. Big-box retailers that already employ pharmacists and offer optometry and audiology services also are moving further into healthcare delivery. COVID-19 tests and vaccinations made the delivery of healthcare in retail settings more familiar and compelling.

As large corporations become more involved in more widely distributed healthcare delivery, they will inevitably exploit technology to cut costs. They will use AI to replace medical specialists in dermatology, radiology, pathology, and any field where AI pattern recognition can provide the same or better diagnoses than physicians do. Dermatologists already can examine lesions from afar using video. A properly trained practitioner can get a sample—a biopsy on a microscope slide that can be scanned by an optical sensor attached to a computer that is underpinned by appropriate machine-learning algorithms to recognize cancers. Specialist physicians don't tend to see themselves being replaced that way anytime soon, but the technology is developing very quickly and may be tested, validated, and implemented faster than they expect. At my hospital network, we regularly engage with companies seeking to set up AI-related research projects.

Healthcare Workplace Changes

The use of AI in medicine further necessitates rethinking what healthcare providers do, how and where they do it, and who gets paid for what. Some jobs will disappear, and new ones will be created. Someone must oversee the AI and make sure inappropriate biases aren't introduced, which is a big problem with today's early AI technology. Healthcare equity already is a burning issue with huge gaps between haves and have-nots, so the last thing we need from technology is to introduce more disparities. Algorithms trained on data that underrepresent some people by gender, race, ethnicity, geography, or other demographics cannot be expected to perform as well for those groups. But the problem goes further, three doctors wrote in *Scientific American*: "Bias in AI is a complex issue; simply providing diverse training data does not guarantee elimination of bias. Several other concerns have been raised—for example, lack of diversity among developers and funders of AI tools; framing of problems from the perspective of majority groups; implicitly biased assumptions about data; and use of outputs of AI tools to perpetuate biases, either inadvertently or explicitly."[42] A human role also is crucial to seeing an AI-produced diagnosis in the context of a full understanding of the patient's situation. Somebody must have enough of a relationship with the patient to ask about family or social support or whatever is needed to deal with the diagnosis, and that person may not be a doctor.

People needing healthcare already are gravitating to whatever outlet is most convenient—calling on-demand telehealth services and visiting urgent care centers or drugstore clinics. In the United States, their health insurance companies are pushing these cost-effective alternatives. Eventually, people may show up at the office of their primary care provider with a whole medical history that the doctor wasn't involved with diagnosing or treating. The doctor can either accept that situation or try to verify everything at the risk of unnecessary and inefficient duplication of services. Healthcare delivery must adapt to this changing patient trajectory by improving the accessibility of medical

---

42   Amit Kaushal, Russ Altman, and Curt Langlotz, "Health Care AI Systems Are Biased," Scientific American, November 17, 2020, https://www.scientificamerican. com/article/health-care-ai-systems-are-biased.

records while still guarding their privacy. Just as important, physicians must accept that they will no longer dictate the patient's trajectory.

Physicians' loss of control over healthcare delivery is interrelated with how they are paid. Those who own their own practices tend to be paid on a fee-for-service basis. For example, a family doctor who spends a lot of time examining someone vulnerable to complex chronic disease could earn a lot more spending the same time on several routine visits with young, healthy people. Because fee-for-service rewards doctors based on volume, not outcome, there has been a movement to adopt value-based payment systems. In the United Kingdom and in Ontario, Canada, doctors are paid a lump sum for each patient treated. This "capitation" system promotes efficiency by not incentivizing unnecessary services. In Quebec, our general practitioners have committed to treating more patients, starting with the most vulnerable, using interdisciplinary teams. Compensation would shift from fee-for-service to a lump sum, depending on the degree of patient vulnerability.[43] That payment system would encourage doctors to take on the complex medical tasks and delegate to allied professionals the more routine work, such as prescription renewals or supporting people with anxiety.

I believe we are moving toward people getting the right care by the right provider in the right place at the right time. But there will be a lot of angst among physicians and some confusion among patients before we get to that point. What is most important is that we end up with the right outcomes.

---

43 Stéphanie Grammond, "Payons les Medécins Autrement," La Presse, May 4, 2022, https://www.lapresse.ca/debats/editoriaux/2022-05-04/payons-les-medecins-autrement.php

Wasted Resources and Care Variation

Decentralization of healthcare delivery may result in some duplication of services, but as we noted in chapter 5, it also has some potential to eliminate part of the waste that researchers estimate accounts for a quarter of US healthcare spending. Policymakers have worked hard for years to tamp down some of the most wasteful practices, such as use of hospital emergency rooms for routine care. Facilities that accommodate procedure-based specialties, such as surgery and gastroenterology, are increasingly using technology to make scheduling more efficient and improve access. Operating rooms sitting unused epitomize wasted resources. A computer program dictating to surgeons when they can use an operating room, on the other hand, is the epitome of devolution of control and will not be warmly welcomed by my colleagues.

A lot of the waste in the system nowadays results from what's called care variation, mostly generated by physicians. Unwarranted variation in healthcare delivery is variation that cannot be explained on the basis of illness, medical evidence, or patient preference, Dr. John Wennberg wrote in the book *Tracking Medicine*.[44] Traditionally, the practice of medicine has been more art than science, with a lot of decision-making—about treatments, tests, devices, and drugs—taking place in gray areas. Sometimes we lack the knowledge to have developed clear standards, and other times physicians choose to ignore clear, evidence-based standards. A classic example involved unwarranted prescriptions of antibiotics in cases where they would have no more effect than a placebo. The resulting waste of resources may have seemed trivial to the doctors, but multiplied across the entire population, it amounted to billions of dollars. Another example is when advertising convinces a patient to ask if a much more expensive drug is

---

44   J. E. Wennberg, Tracking Medicine (New York: Oxford University Press, 2010), 4.

right for them, and the doctor agrees to the prescription because that patient's insurance covers it. As policymakers pay more attention to reducing care variation, doctors may lose that liberty, as has happened with various rules and regulations compelling use of generic drugs.

We are going from guidelines in the practice of medicine to expecting doctors to follow a standardized approach for a particular type of patient and condition. Physicians can make a case that some patients need to be the exception to the rule, but most patients will do fine if the physicians stick to the order set, which is designed to reduce cost, improve quality of care, and improve access. In the big picture of what we all want healthcare to be, those three goals are interrelated. Having all the members of the team using the same playbook facilitates an intelligent continuum of care everywhere the patient goes.

The Right Care, But Where?

Culture and tradition play a role in what happens where in healthcare delivery. For many women these days, the right place to give birth is in a hospital with an obstetrician ready to handle any worst-case scenarios. My health network also has birthing centers outside the hospital that are run by midwives. It's a very European practice and preferred by a portion of the population in Quebec. But occasionally a delivery has complications a midwife can't handle, and the patient is urgently transferred to our hospital. Obstetricians who suddenly must take responsibility for a delivery they didn't initiate with a patient they never met can be exasperated. Of course, midwives existed long before doctors and then obstetricians took over deliveries over the past 150 years. And now we're slowly moving back to where obstetricians deal only with high-risk individuals or with complications of other people's attempted deliveries. Family physicians in training in a hospital must learn how to do deliveries, so that makes a three-way competition for control in obstetrics.

In contrast, the Royal College of Physicians and Surgeons of Canada does not expect the orthopedic surgeons it is responsible for certifying to be competent to look after their patients' postoperative (nonsurgical) medical problems, so it's not part of their training. That's a perplexing difference from how I was trained as a general surgeon, but as a hospital administrator, I must ensure someone goes into the orthopedic ward to care for those patients. After a lot of angst, family doctors agreed to function as hospitalists in that role, which makes sense because of their broad-based training.

Another trend affecting where people get care is the rising importance of what other industries would call the customer experience. Consumers are increasingly shopping online for healthcare services and relying on posted reviews to select primary care. A 2021 survey of US adults found most would be unlikely to see a provider with less than four stars in online reviews even if another provider had referred them.[45] The preceding examples ranging from obstetrics to orthopedics to more routine primary care all reflect how we are adjusting the roles of physicians in the evolving next generation of healthcare.

The Inevitable Disintermediation

Disintermediation has become a familiar part of our digital lives, as we discussed near the beginning of this book. We can skip a visit to a banker, a broker, or even a car dealership and complete our transactions directly by ourselves online without an intermediary. Similar

---

45   Deb Gordon, "Is the Era Of Healthcare Consumerism Finally Here? New Survey Says Yes," Forbes, December. 2, 2021, https://www.forbes.com/sites/debgordon/2021/12/02/is-the-era-of-healthcare-consumerism-finally-here-new-survey-says-yes/?sh=61b8c4483840.

disintermediation is the logical consequence of the devolution of control in healthcare.

Disintermediation is inevitable in healthcare wherever it is more efficient and cost-effective. When people are comfortable getting diagnoses, therapeutics, or any other care without a physician, they will do so. Physicians may resist participating in systemic change that provides them no payoff, but society will move on. More doctors will be hospital employees, fewer will be their own boss, and they may be unhappy with that status. Physicians on salary must have some quotas or incentives to maintain productivity, and that makes them feel less in control. But people's sympathy is limited for a group that traditionally has been very well paid. In some cases, technology or automation frees medical professionals' time so they can focus on higher-value tasks. But that rosy outcome usually doesn't happen without some friction and adjustment. In the case of the hospital-at-home program described in chapter 3, I heard from physicians concerned they had no billing code to be paid for the requisite virtual visits. This type of issue seems to be happening around the world and must be addressed quickly, most likely by deploying salaried nurse practitioners or advanced-practice nurses to handle any virtual care that doesn't require a physician. The tradeoff with that solution is decreasing the time those nurses are available in hospital wards or assisting doctors in face-to-face care. As of December 2022, a billing code was in fact created by the government to allow specialist physicians to bill for services provided in our hospital@home program.

> **Physicians may resist participating in systemic change that provides them no payoff, but society will move on.**

The cost-effectiveness of disintermediation is not only about automating work or shifting it to lower-paid people, it also must involve moving care upstream by making it more preventive and preemptive. Wellness-related interventions make for fewer people downstream with the chronic medical issues that need a physician's intervention. It has long been obvious that many of the most common and expensive medical issues are lifestyle related. Paying more attention to exercise, nutrition, and other social determinants of healthcare is a critically important part of cost control.

Patient-centered wellness programs that bring new players and self-administered devices into healthcare inevitably change workloads and disempower some medical professionals. To put it in a more familiar way, they will be getting a smaller slice of the healthcare spending pie. In my experience, those on the verge of losing control often react with disbelief or denial, though it should be obvious that change is inevitable. But progress that saves time and effort can add up to the elimination of some people's jobs, including physicians, and the creation of new jobs.

FREEDOM FROM THE BEEPER

When I started practicing transplant surgery at Montreal General Hospital in 1987, the standard way to summon a doctor was with a pager. For readers too young to recall these rudimentary wireless devices, the earliest ones just beeped. Then the person being paged would have to find a landline telephone, call the paging operator, and find out who was paging and what number to call them at. Being unsatisfied with this technological marvel, I was the first hospital staffer to get the newer model that had a small alphanumeric display to show the caller's phone number. So began the disintermediation that led to the happy day when I was able to ditch the pager and pioneer use of a cellular telephone, where those whom I gave my number could call me directly.

Large institutions have the resources to update to the latest technology, but they do it at their own bureaucratic pace, unless someone is pushing them. My nature is that once I know there's a better way, I want to know how I can get there. In the case of the alphanumeric pager, I had to buy it myself and then persuade the hospital to allow me to use it. As other people started seeing it, they wanted the same thing, and eventually they got it. The jump to the cellphone also began with me buying my own, and it took even longer to become standard issue. As director of the surgical research program at the hospital, testing new technology seemed to me to fall within my departmental mission, but bringing unfamiliar devices to work carried a touch of eccentricity.

Trillion-Dollar Possibilities

A related disintermediation involves the entry of large technology corporations into aspects of healthcare delivery that have been the domain of governments. Six tech companies see trillion-dollar possibilities in healthcare, Dr. Bertalan Meskó wrote in 2021 in his magazine *The Medical Futurist*. He noted how the big tech companies each have something unique to offer—Amazon contributing its distribution network, Microsoft powering predictable enterprise IT, Apple designing seamless systems with its apps and wearable devices, Google applying AI, IBM providing computing power and machine learning, and NVIDIA knowing how to manufacture systems and practical implementations.[46] The tech companies are establishing a digital infrastructure in healthcare just as they did in other industries.

Outpaced government regulators can be left in the dust, but the bigger picture is that the companies, rather than the government, increasingly provide an organizing principle to structure the provision of healthcare. For example, in my province of Canada, we have a publicly funded system of hospitals in which the government historically has accepted that the doctors are independent contractors who bargain for compensation, work rules, and benefits through their unions. The United States has different federal and state structures underlying its medical establishment, with its eclectic mix of public and private health insurance. Companies emerged decades ago to help administer prescription plans for US health insurance companies, and after a lot of mergers and acquisitions, three huge pharmacy-benefit managers play a powerful role in US healthcare. How the tech companies will influence the medical establishment is still unfolding. Considering how much of what doctors do has changed over the years, there can be no doubt change will accelerate as tech companies develop algorithms that match or exceed the capabilities of medical specialists. AI will be pervasive throughout healthcare, not just in therapeutics and diagnostics but also increasingly in processes and management. It is not hard to imagine at least one tech giant acquiring a large healthcare system—if it hasn't already happened by the time you are reading this.

---

46   Dr. Bertalan Meskó, "Big Tech in Medicine: How Amazon, Apple, Microsoft, Google, IBM & NVIDIA Disrupt Healthcare," The Medical Futurist, August 24, 2021, https://medicalfuturist.com/tech-giants-in-healthcare-2021-summary.

Circling Back

The need to rethink what healthcare providers do, how and where they do it, and who gets paid for what is already apparent will only grow as AI capabilities develop further. Healthcare delivery must confront its problem of wasted resources because decentralization could lead to more duplication. In looking for cost savings, administrators are targeting unwarranted care variation and pushing physicians to hew to data-driven, evidence-based standards. The consequence of taking control away from doctors is that patients have more control—and responsibility—for managing their own healthcare. What if patients replace physicians in what we described at the beginning of this chapter as "the top of the food chain"? If those patients already have high blood pressure or diabetes, they can decide how and where to monitor and treat their condition. Big tech corporations will be pervasive in the new healthcare landscape because they can offer convenient, efficient solutions with the promise of cost effectiveness. But the challenge for society in achieving cost-effective healthcare is making people interested in taking control of their wellness to prevent chronic illnesses. In the chapters ahead, we will examine the consequences of disintermediation and the dangers lurking in a system that provides care everywhere. Whether you are a policymaker or just someone personally concerned about healthcare, what protections and precautions are needed for the future?

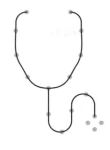

CHAPTER 9

Moving toward Sustainability

The host on Canada's public television network began his show with an alarming statistic: the latest Ontario health data showed the average wait time in hospital emergency rooms was 20 hours before a patient got a bed. Even more stunning was the caption superimposed as he began interviewing the head of the country's largest association of doctors: "Canada's healthcare system on the verge of collapse, says head of CMA." No matter where you were during the COVID-19 pandemic, you surely heard stories about hospital staff shortages and healthcare worker burnout. "Collapse" became a common descriptor of healthcare's struggle amid the pandemic, from Washington to Rio de Janeiro to Mumbai. But when this segment aired it was June 2022 and Dr. Katharine Smart, president of the Canadian Medical Association, was warning on a political news show that things were still bad and getting worse:

Our emergency departments are overwhelmed. We've got people waiting sometimes 18, 24 hours to be seen, elders sitting on gurneys for days waiting to be admitted to hospital. We're short-staffed. We can't actually get people care. We've got growing backlogs. This means real people waiting sometimes years to have essential surgeries, things that allow them to go to work, be around their families. And then in the backdrop, primary care falling apart, even worse than before, you know, before the pandemic, we already had five million Canadians without access to that front door of the healthcare system. That's getting worse by the day. We're seeing more and more people raising the alarm that they can't carry on, they're leaving their family practice. So I think when the healthcare system's really no longer able to provide care to patients in a timely way, that to me means it's starting to collapse.[47]

Health provider trade groups and regulators in the US sounded similar alarms. *Healthcare Finance*, a trade publication, reported in October 2021 that after more than a year and a half of dealing with COVID-19, US hospital employee turnover had increased to nearly 20 percent, five times higher than the general workforce.[48] Burnout from the pandemic was just one issue squeezing the healthcare job market. As many dif-

> People in under-served areas wait far too long to see specialists.

---

47 Katharine Smart, Power & Politics, CBC News, interview by David Cochrane, June 17, 2022, https://www.cbc.ca/player/play/2044498499884.

48 Jeff Lagasse, "Hospitals Pay High Turnover Costs Due to RNs Leaving the Profession," Healthcare Finance, October 15, 2021, https://www.healthcarefinancenews.com/news/hospitals-pay-high-turnover-costs-due-rns-leaving-profession.

ferences as there are in the healthcare systems in Canada, the United States, and other countries, they all have sustainability challenges that preceded the pandemic. People in underserved areas wait far too long to see specialists. Rural hospitals or their emergency rooms have closed because of staff shortages. Even in large cities, people must wait too long for surgeries.

Someone I know quite well told me that his urologist decided he needed to be checked every six months for an early stage prostate cancer. But his first follow-up appointment got pushed back two months without explanation, even though he already had gotten a blood test with troublesome results. I found out the urologist was unaware of this, as he was too busy covering for three colleagues who were out sick. But the reasons for delays in care are not usually so straightforward.

Robyn Urback, a columnist for the *Globe and Mail* newspaper in Toronto, astutely observed how the system could be so broken: "There is no one solution because the problems are multidimensional. Family doctors in Canada are overworked and underpaid, meaning fewer medical students are choosing family medicine. As a result of the shortage of family doctors, those without primary care often end up in emergency rooms, exacerbating hospital wait times. When people (usually elderly) are too sick to go home but not really sick enough to stay in hospital, they remain there, contributing to overcrowding because we don't have enough rehab facilities, transitory living spaces or long-term care homes to accommodate them."[49]

Systems developed in which society paid for healthcare based on volume of services delivered, even as costs ballooned. Applying a more

---

49   Robyn Urback, "Canadians Are Delusional Captives to a Broken Health Care System," Globe and Mail, July 14, 2022, https://www.theglobeandmail.com/opinion/article-canadians-are-delusional-captives-to-a-broken-health-care-system.

businesslike approach of measuring outcomes and the value we get for the money we spend helps us see why what we have been doing is not sustainable. The democratization of technology that we discussed in chapter 7 promises some relief but creates tensions between the self-regulating culture of big tech and the legacy systems in which governments, licensing boards, and insurers have staked out their control over healthcare delivery.

Who Makes the Standards?

The entry of large technology corporations into healthcare delivery raises the prospect that they, not governments, will set standards. We have seen governments pull back from regulating the telecommunications and entertainment industries. Landline phone companies were highly regulated, but wireless companies mostly set their own standards beyond being told what bandwidths they can use. Broadcast television had to mind its manners and watch its language for fear of government fines, but cable television and the Web staked their claim in an anything-goes frontier. The more pervasive megacorporations become in healthcare, the less ground is left for government to control.

As we discussed in chapter 2, healthcare is a "complex adaptive system," so in addition to having complex rules that vary from place to place and keep changing, it also has individual agents interacting in unpredictable and paradoxical ways. Some familiar examples illustrate this point. Both the United States and Canada have programs called Medicare, and they are quite different. In Canada, 13 provincial and territorial governments are responsible for managing and delivering publicly funded healthcare to their residents. In the United States, healthcare is largely a for-profit business, but people turning 65 years old can apply for a single-payer Medicare, and they can buy supplemental insurance from private companies, with or without a program called Medicare Advantage that subsidizes the insurers to serve as intermediaries between the government and the beneficiaries. Both the Canadian and US governments impose complicated rules and standards and cap reimbursement rates to keep their publicly funded programs afloat financially. The US private insurers and providers must adjust to protect their profits while complying with the rules, and it is not unusual for an insurer to drop a doctor from a Medicare Advantage plan or for a healthcare provider to opt out of taking Medicare patients.

For individuals, a healthcare system fulfills their expectations only if they can purchase what they need. If they are in the United Kingdom, for example, many services are free through the single-payer National Health Service, but the law of supply and demand governs availability, and rising costs inevitably lead to service reductions. In the United States, individuals who are not eligible for employer-sponsored private health insurance or Medicare are supposed to be able to afford care through Obamacare, which also includes the federally subsidized Medicaid program, which is state-administered and often delivered through private managed-care programs for low-income recipients. Taking advantage of these programs requires individuals to enroll, and they often must pay some confusing combination of premiums, deductibles, and copayments when they are approved to receive services. These hurdles and barriers did not appear by accident. They were erected to keep healthcare sustainable in the face of rapidly rising costs.

Something Needs to Change

The total amount of public and private money spent on healthcare has taken up an increasing share of the value of all goods and services, with the rise especially steep in the United States. The percentage of US gross domestic product going to health was 5 percent in 1960, nearly 9 percent in 1980, and more than 17 percent from 2009 to 2019. It shot up to 19.7 percent in 2020 with the pandemic.[50] But even in 2018, the US Centers for Disease Control reported, the country was spending $3.6 trillion on health, which was $11,172 per capita.[51] Behind that average are equity issues, because while high-income households naturally spend more in dollars on everything, including health, people who are poorer and sicker spend a much higher percentage of their income on healthcare. Pharmaceutical prices are a particular issue in the US, with persistent stories about financially stretched people not filling prescriptions or skipping doses. In Canada and Europe, access to timely care is a larger concern.

As we discussed in chapters 3 and 8, wasteful care variation contributes to the high cost. The Fraser Institute, which is a think tank in Canada, compared the performance of 28 universal-access healthcare systems among countries in the Organization for Economic Co-operation and Development (OECD). This annual comparison is highly regarded because of the way it sheds light on the value we are getting from the money we spend, and how we might improve it. The provision of healthcare is measured using 40 indicators, representing four broad categories:

1. availability of resources,
2. use of resources,
3. access to resources, and

---

50   Statista Research Department, "U.S. National Health Expenditure as Percent of GDP from 1960 to 2020," July 27, 2022, https://www.statista.com/statistics/184968/us-health-expenditure-as-percent-of-gdp-since-1960.

51   "Health Expenditures," National Center for Health Statistics, Centers for Disease Control and Prevention, accessed December 11, 2022, https://www.cdc.gov/nchs/fastats/health-expenditures.htm.

4. clinical performance and quality.

Five indicators measuring the overall health status of the population are also included. These indicators, such as life expectancy and mortality rates, may be determined more by nonmedical factors, such as access to clean water and good nutrition, but help complete the picture of how a country's healthcare system is performing. The conclusion:

> "Canada ranks among the most expensive universal health-care systems in the OECD. However, its performance for availability and access to resources is generally below that of the average OECD country, while its performance for use of resources and quality and clinical performance is mixed. Clearly, there is an imbalance between the value Canadians receive and the relatively high amount of money they spend on their health-care system."[52]

Some countries, like Japan, have older populations than other countries, like Israel, and healthcare spending rises with age, so the researchers adjusted data by age for comparability. They noted that in 2016, seniors over 65 years old represented 17 percent of the Canadian population but consumed 45 percent of all healthcare expenditures. Another Fraser Institute report showed how the aging population affects expenditures. Without policy changes, it concluded, Canadians over the age of 65 will account for more than 70 percent of expenditures on basic healthcare by 2040.[53] A lot of factors and assumptions

---

52   Mackenzie Moir and Bacchus Barua, "Comparing Performance of Universal Health Care Countries, 2021," Fraser Institute, accessed December 11, 2022, https://www.fraserinstitute.org/sites/default/files/comparing-performance-universal-health-care-countries-2021.pdf.

53   Steven Globerman, "Aging and Expenditures on Health Care," Fraser Research Bulletin (March 2021).

go into producing these trend lines, but the main ones are that seniors are living longer and that demographic bulges, like the baby boom, lead to expanded and expensive end-of-life care.

The population of care providers is aging along with the patients. As a baby boomer, I'm at an age when many of my professional colleagues have already retired or are about to retire. As a hiring manager, I can see there are not enough people out there to replace us—even in Canada and the US, which are a magnet for highly educated immigrants. The World Health Organization estimates a projected shortfall of 15 million health workers by 2030, mostly in low- and lower-middle-income countries.[54]

NO DOCTOR, BIG PROBLEM

I stopped in a bakery recently where the woman behind the counter knows what I do for a living because she has seen me interviewed frequently on television. She asked me if I could find her a doctor. I said, "It's really quite tough. I can try to see what I can do." She said, "I haven't had a doctor in ten years and neither has anyone in my family." They were longtime residents of Montreal, where the public healthcare system should cover anyone being able to go to a doctor. The issue was not affordability, it was lack of access due to a shortage of family physicians. The government has tried to set up a referral helpline for people to call, but even if there were enough doctors for the "orphaned patients," there is a shortage of nurses or others with the training and experience to triage the callers.

---

54   "Health Workforce," World Health Organization, accessed December 11, 2022, https://www.who.int/health-topics/health-workforce#tab=tab_1.

Being without a primary-care doctor may not be a big issue for people who are perfectly healthy, but for others, it is a real concern. Any country that doesn't provide all its residents with a foundational level of healthcare is just going to push people's health problems downstream, where they will become more expensive to care for, intensifying the sustainability challenges.

What Can Change?

Healthcare is not immune from the law of supply and demand, but it doesn't respond very flexibly to those forces. Rigid and complex requirements exist for training and licensing medical providers. Because the requirements vary by jurisdiction, human resources cannot be shifted around the country or world to meet needs as easily as it is done by corporations in other industries. Training additional physicians is very expensive, and whoever is paying for it—in some countries like Canada, the government—may not be willing to devote the resources. It took more than a decade for Canada to catch up when it allowed crippling shortages of certain medical specialties to occur in the early 1990s, and it is happening again. The Association of American Medical Colleges (AAMC) projected in June 2020 that the US faces a shortfall of between 54,100 and 139,000 physicians by 2033. Its annual surveys of its members found that enrollment in the nation's medical schools was growing, but there was increasing competition for the residency programs and clinical training sites where students complete their requirements to become medical doctors. Demand for training was growing, especially in obstetrics/gynecology, pediatrics, and family medicine, but federal funding was not keeping pace, the AAMC reported.[55]

We have discussed the trend in which general practitioners are doing work previously performed by specialty physicians and nurse practitioners, pharmacists, or other allied healthcare professionals are gaining the skills and permission to take on higher-level tasks. The trend is unstoppable because it is a cost-effective approach in the long run, but not so fast or pervasive in the short run because it is subject to the increased competition for training resources. Private investors will put capital into developing AI to substitute for humans in providing certain types of interventions or care surveillance, but it will take time to become widely accepted enough to make a difference. Another promising but gradual trend toward more sustainability in healthcare involves redirecting resources upstream toward wellness and disease prevention. Trends in fitness and nutrition may not be directly connected to medicine but affect healthcare sustainability. So do people's feelings about living wills, hospice, and even immigration policy, which helps determine the age distribution in a national population.

Paying for Outcomes

As mentioned in chapter 2, influential research at Harvard Business School that started more than 15 years ago showed the need for a strategy to maximize value to patients by achieving the best outcomes and the lowest costs. Professor Michael Porter and his colleagues made a convincing case for restructuring how healthcare delivery is organized, measured, and reimbursed:

---

55   Patrick Boyle, "Medical School Enrollments Grow, But Residency Slots Haven't Kept Pace," AAMC News, September 3, 2020, https://www.aamc.org/news-insights/medical-school-enrollments-grow-residency-slots-haven-t-kept-pace.

"We must move away from a supply-driven health care system organized around what physicians do and toward a patient-centered system organized around what patients need. We must shift the focus from the volume and profitability of services provided—physician visits, hospitalizations, procedures, and tests—to the patient outcomes achieved. And we must replace today's fragmented system, in which every local provider offers a full range of services, with a system in which services for particular medical conditions are concentrated in health-delivery organizations and in the right locations to deliver high-value care."[56]

Porter's seminal work led to the creation of the International Consortium of Health Outcome Measurement (ICHOM). The Boston-based nonprofit organization provides a platform for healthcare providers to benchmark outcomes with standardized, validated measurements. At its heart, the approach envisions, in Porter's words, "a world where patients ask their doctors about meaningful outcomes, and doctors can respond with data-driven answers."[57]

At an early ICHOM meeting several years ago, I saw a touching video that cut to the essence of the value-based approach and its reliance on patient-reported outcome measures. A lung-cancer patient in the video was asked what he wanted to result from his cancer therapy. He didn't respond like a physician with talk about survival rates and the comparative risks and side-effects of surgery, chemotherapy, and radiation treatments. He didn't say how long he hoped to live or how pain-free. He said what he wanted from the treatment was to be able to

---

56   Michael E. Porter and Thomas H. Lee, "The Strategy That Will Fix Health Care," Harvard Business Review, October 2013, 3.

57   "Hear from Michael Porter on Ichom's History, Strategy and Structure," May 2020, https://www.ichom.org/mission/.

blow the trumpet again for his grandson. People in the audience were visibly moved. But when I retold the story as a speaker at a later conference on value-based healthcare, a doctor stood up from the audience and screamed about how absurd he found the story. Others in the audience were dumbstruck by his reaction, but it reflected the lack of acceptance by some doctors of a patient-centric ethos.

A Lesson from the Past

Doctors in training went on strike in the early 1980s in Quebec, where collective agreements govern pay and working hours. Residents and interns walked out of the hospitals, except the surgical residents. I was a senior general surgery resident at my hospital at the time and was on duty one night covering the emergency department for surgery when I got called over by an attending physician who was a faculty member in internal medicine. Normally he would have residents looking after patients and performing procedures that I realized he hadn't done himself in many years. Suddenly it was his job to put tubes in people's chests or insert central venous catheters, and he needed it to become my job that night. Although he was nonetheless an excellent physician in his own right, the acute-care skills he had acquired 25 years earlier were not maintained. I didn't want to end up like that, being almost useless in an acute-care setting.

Hospital reliance on residents working long hours at low pay has been a simmering issue for many years. It comes to public attention when there is news coverage of a death being blamed on a resident or doctor on call being exhausted by working too many hours. In one famous case, 18-year-old Libby Zion died at a prominent New York City teaching hospital after being evaluated and treated with various drugs by junior medical residents who consulted by phone with a medical intern who was covering multiple wards.[58] Libby was the daughter of a prominent newspaper columnist and former prosecutor, Sidney Zion, who sued for malpractice and persuaded the district attorney to convene a grand jury that issued a critical report. I don't believe the number of hours the attending doctor was on call was to blame for the death, which involved drug interactions, but residents, among others, have taken the story to heart. The long hours never bothered me when I was a resident. I figured it was sort of like going through boot camp in the military—you do it only once and should make the most of the preparation before you end up on the battlefield. But the lesson for dealing with today's sustainability challenges in healthcare is not to make everyone work harder, putting in more hours. We must work smarter and keep polishing our skills so we can adapt to changing roles and take advantage of new technology.

SPECIALIZATION ISSUES

As we have become increasingly specialized in medicine, we run into situations where the right person is not available and whoever is available doesn't feel right about taking on the task. Surgeons of a certain age may not feel competent to do procedures they would have done five or 10 years earlier. Anesthetists as they age are less comfortable dealing with certain situations, especially when they are called upon late at night. Technology may help. For example, robotic-assisted surgery can provide more precise control to counteract the tremor some of us develop as we age, and it allows us to operate on patients whom we might

---

58   Marc K. Wallack and Lynn Chao, "Resident Work Hours: The Evolution of a Revolution," The Archives of Surgery 136, no. 12 (2001):1426–32, https://doi.org/10.1001/archsurg.136.12.1426.

not otherwise have operated on because they were too old, frail, or morbidly obese. That's a good thing for those people but adds to the workload amid staffing shortages.

Some Policy Interventions

Many countries with national healthcare restrict whether physicians can practice outside the public system or how much they can do so. But that doesn't necessarily mean there are enough doctors. Where I live in Quebec, the government is supposed to use a permit system to equitably allocate doctors across the province. When the government transferred some primary-care positions from the island of Montreal in 2021 to suburban areas where there are long waits to enroll with a family doctor, many people both in and out of the healthcare system were upset. The health minister blamed Montreal doctors for not working enough.[59] To be sure, the population of doctors is aging, and some older doctors slow down and refuse to take after-hours calls. Some young doctors spend more time with their initial patients, but my observation in Montreal is that most primary-care physicians build a practice of about 1,500 people and work at least 45 or 50 hours a week.

In private practice, doctors can limit the number of patients they will see and offer exclusive services for an annual fee, an arrangement mostly known in the US as concierge medicine. Patients may get

---

59 Selena Ross and Rob Lurie, "Quebec Minister Says Montreal Family Doctors Don't Work Enough, Shifts New Jobs to Suburbs," CTV News, October 8, 2021, https://montreal.ctvnews.ca/quebec-minister-says-montreal-family-doctors-don-t-work-enough-shifts-new-jobs-to-suburbs-1.5616861.

more time and attention, and the doctors may find the work less of a grind, but it means fewer primary-care physicians available to those who can't pay the membership fee. Israel has struck a nice balance and gotten good rankings on international performance indicators. Israel's nationally funded medical insurance plan mandates all its resident citizens join one of four HMOs. The HMOs require that physicians give them a set number of hours per week. After that, they are free to work in private practice, where they can earn more money seeing people willing to pay extra for more services or amenities.

Policymakers in every country require or incentivize some commitment to whatever public healthcare system they have, out of fear that nobody would work in it otherwise. I don't know of any evidence bearing out that concern. The United States presents a prime example of how much wasteful spending can result from having nearly unlimited opportunities for private healthcare delivery. The outcomes used to benchmark performance are far lower in the US than in some European countries that spend a lot smaller share of their GDP on healthcare. At the outset of the pandemic in 2020, when stay-at-home orders were financially crippling medical providers, the US Congress authorized a $178 billion bailout that kept hospitals and physician practices afloat, but that wealth was transferred only to big, for-profit hospitals.[60]

A 2020 Harris Poll survey of US adults commissioned by a data analytics company called Change Healthcare found that half said they avoided seeking care because the system is too hard to deal with. The pain points involved access to care and the lack of transparency in

---

60 Christopher Rowland, "The Unintended Consequences of the $178 Billion Bailout to Keep Hospitals and Doctors Afloat," Washington Post, June 22, 2022, https://www. washingtonpost.com/business/2022/06/22/covid-hospital-relief-fund.

costs.[61] In the US system, people sometimes don't know until months after a healthcare visit what they will be billed. Consultants say one in three patients admit ignoring bills they can't understand. Listening to patients and reorganizing healthcare around the outcomes they seek is the best strategy for making the system sustainable.

Circling Back

Around the world, societies developed healthcare systems that paid providers based on the volume of services they delivered. These systems are all struggling in different ways with shortfalls of human and financial resources to keep up with demand. Governments and private intermediaries, such as insurance companies, have propped up the systems with regulations and limits that are reaching the end of their sustainability. Failing to prevent and treat medical conditions only leads to more costs downstream. Healthcare has been taking up an increasing share of our economic resources for years, reaching crisis levels during COVID-19.

The pandemic also brought home to healthcare providers the need to be more consumer friendly when their revenue was hit by people skipping routine visits and turning to telehealth. The convenience of telehealth won over a lot of people and forced legacy healthcare providers to face up to how far behind other industries they were in using digital communications—text reminders, online scheduling, and tools to shop for services. People already annoyed by long wait times for appointments and lack of price clarity were increasingly

---

61　Change Healthcare, "Harris Poll Research: Half of Consumers Avoid Seeking Care Because It's Too Hard," changehealthcare.com, July 13, 2020, https://ir.changehealthcare.com/news-releases/news-release-details/change-healthcare-harris-poll-research-half-consumers-avoid.

willing to try something new, like telehealth or store-based clinics, which we will discuss in the pages ahead.

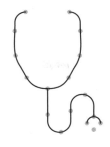

CHAPTER 10

Virtual Care—Not In-Person but Still Personal

Ido Schoenberg, chairman and co-CEO of Amwell, a Boston-based telehealth company that operates throughout the US, recalls how his company's founders were inspired by the retail sector's success moving consumers into online interactions. Schoenberg told the McKinsey consulting firm for a 2021 report that after the company was founded in 2006, the Amwell leaders realized there were many discouraging barriers to healthcare having similar success. They spent three months in a room with lots of whiteboards and "despite the fact that the room was filled with red ink," they still underestimated the challenges:

> Making telehealth safe, making it legal in different states in the United States, building enough evidence to show that telehealth should be a covered benefit, getting the doctor comfortable treating patients far away, getting people comfortable knowing they can get care online,

making this entire thing simple at a time when we still had USB cameras that we had to connect to our computers and learn those systems. These things were so complicated back then! Today, people largely don't think twice about video conferencing.

The biggest challenge of all is psychological, and in some respects, I don't think we have completely overcome these challenges. There is magic in the physical interaction between doctor and patient, especially in times of great fear, or great need, and technology is not completely there yet. But we are working really hard to make sure we get as close as possible so we can provide a lot of value.[62]

It may go without saying, but Schoenberg emphasized that telehealth was never intended to replace all physical interaction because some things can only be done in person. This chapter will discuss the promises and limitations of virtual care in all its variations. Any healthcare interaction that doesn't transpire directly face to face in the same physical space is, by definition, virtual care. This may involve people simply consulting their own doctor by telephone for primary care or finding an app or service online to gauge or manage chronic health concerns. A fast-growing business sector offers on-call providers for urgent acute care. Particularly in the United States, health insurers will partner with a virtual-care enterprise to give their customers more care access. Some programs like the hospital at home we discussed earlier have a hub facility, like our command center, that performs remote monitoring using digital devices handled by patients or their

---

62   Ido Schoenberg, "How Health Tech Can Democratize Healthcare," interview by Ulrike Deetjen, McKinsey & Company, June 2021, https://www.mckinsey.com/industries/healthcare-systems-and-services/our-insights/how-health-tech-can-democratize-healthcare-an-interview-with-ido-schoenberg.

family members. Hub facilities also could send trained caregivers to people's homes or ask rural patients to visit a nearby clinic as an intermediary to help them be examined virtually by a specialist in a remote city. In addition to all these real-time connections, virtual care can be asynchronous, with information uploaded into a secure web portal, or in situations where it is acceptable, using email, text messages, voicemail, or fax.

The Pandemic as a Motivator

While some aspects of virtual care date back many years, COVID-19 forced much wider adoption. Data scientists in the United States created a Telehealth Adoption Tracker, which showed that virtual care usage peaked in the second quarter of 2020, but after significantly declining, it remained higher than prepandemic levels.[63] Surveys by Advisory Board showed the percentage of American adults who would consider virtual care in different scenarios increased from half or less in 2017 to roughly two-thirds in 2020. Postpandemic usage of virtual care has tended to be higher among younger and healthier patients. But most American adults, including half of those younger than the baby boomers, do not want to replace in-person primary care with telehealth entirely, according to a November 2020 Harris Poll.[64]

I mentioned earlier that the main motivation for the almost overnight launch of our hospital-at-home program was concern that another COVID wave would again fill our beds and curtail our capacity to catch up with already delayed non-COVID care. But at the time,

---

63   The Chartis Group and Kythera Labs, "Telehealth Adoption Steadying toward a New Normal Rate," Chartis, September 8, 2021, https://www.chartis.com/insights/telehealth-adoption-tracker.

64   Rebecca Tyrrell, "How Covid-19 Has Changed Consumer Behavior and Preferences," Advisory Board, June 29, 2020, https://www.advisory.com/topics/consumerism/2020/06/covid19-consumer-behavior-and-preferences.

medical centers also were dealing with hundreds of staff members who couldn't come into work. They were sick or were quarantining because they had been exposed to COVID. Many crucial aspects of healthcare, including surgeries and cancer treatments, require having enough of the right human resources in the right place at the right time. Virtual care was able to relieve pressure on our ability to offer those services. When we could put healthcare workers who were sitting at home in quarantine back to work remotely, it was a spectacular win-win. They were happy to pitch in during a worldwide medical crisis rather than collecting sick pay for doing nothing.

Follow the Money

As the pandemic accustomed people to interacting more online and relying more on digital services, venture capitalists detected a rich sector uniquely ripe for disruption, the *Economist* reported in January 2022. The magazine displayed a chart using estimates from CB Insights, a data provider, showing that investments in digital-health startups nearly doubled year-over-year in 2021, to $57 billion. The *Economist* found 90 healthcare startups valued at $1 billion or more not listed on the stock exchanges, and it noted that some large publicly traded pharmaceutical companies, including Johnson & Johnson, were spinning off their consumer-products divisions.[65] News reports suggested the motivation for the spinoffs was that consumer products like J&J's Band-Aids and baby powder were much less profitable than pharmaceuticals. But a more likely explanation is that the

---

65 "How Health Care Is Turning into a Consumer Product," Economist, January 15, 2022, https://www.economist.com/business/how-health-care-is-turning-into-a-consumer-product/21807114. This article appeared in the Business section of the print edition under the headline "Move Fast and Heal Things."

spinoffs will try to compete with the startups and big tech in developing self-monitoring and diagnostic devices for virtual care.

The evidence is obvious that big corporations see what we described in chapter 8 as trillion-dollar possibilities in healthcare. When Google announced in 2019 that it was spending $2.1 billion to acquire Fitbit, it not only was getting into wellness wearables but also acquiring many years of user health data. In June 2022, Oracle Corporation, an American multinational business software and cloud-computing company, completed a $28.3 billion acquisition of Cerner, a provider of digital information systems used within hospitals and health systems. Oracle promised in a news release that it would "make Cerner's systems much easier to learn and use by making hands-free voice technology the primary interface."[66] Not coincidentally, Microsoft acquired Nuance, a leader in voice recognition technology, for $19.7 billion in 2021. Providing care everywhere requires making people's electronic health records easier to produce and access. If doctors can spend less of their time typing on keyboards and more time talking to patients, that's a win-win situation.

Some Cultural Issues Remain

Many patients love the convenience of virtual care, but some people are more resistant than others to new ways of doing things, and that certainly includes physicians. Some physicians have offered specific concerns related to remuneration or medical malpractice issues, which will work themselves out over time as virtual care matures. Healthcare administrators in some places already have begun developing adaptive change-management programs to deal with physician

---

66   Oracle, "Oracle Purchase of Cerner Approved," news release, June 1, 2022, https://www.oracle.com/news/announcement/oracle-purchase-of-cerner-approved-2022-06-01/.

concerns, whether they are real or perceived. Adaptive change refers to the challenge of getting team members on board over an extended time to overcome complicated issues without clear solutions in sight. When asked to participate in virtual care, some physicians have told me they're very happy functioning the way they have in the past and "if it ain't broke don't fix it." Those of us who believe healthcare's business is to serve the people, not the physicians, will move forward with virtual care based on positive user-experience survey results.

Surveys show acceptance of virtual care among patients is not confined to a younger or tech-savvy population. Virtual care is popular with people of any age who have a successful experience using it to

> Ideally, virtual care doesn't just replicate in-person care but is more efficient and allows patients to have more control over their information and treatment.

manage chronic conditions, those who need to see a lot of providers and specialists, and those busy with work or childcare. Some best practices have emerged to ensure that patients are not turned off by a bad experience. Instead of assigning them to virtual care, they can be allowed to choose it or have it recommended to them based on a questionnaire. Accommodation can be made for those who say

they don't have access to the necessary technology or who need technical support. But even the tech-savvy may have bad experiences due to interoperability issues in healthcare providers' legacy systems. A large medical center may be able to pay for a turnkey system from a leading technology corporation, but just as often, we are piecing together a technology infrastructure and relying on small companies that may go out of business, leaving a gap in the patients' electronic health records.

Ideally, virtual care doesn't just replicate in-person care but is more efficient and allows patients to have more control over their information and treatment. Without being experts themselves, people should be able to fill in a questionnaire and have technology, aided by AI, match them to providers, finding the right specialist, pharmacy, or imaging lab, and seamlessly completing the referral and scheduling. This goal comes back to the concept of healthcare becoming more personal. It also extends a growing trend of people searching for providers online and relying on reviews rather than personal recommendations.

AN IPHONE APP GETS IT TOGETHER

In 2018, Apple announced that its Health app for iPhone would be capable of displaying a user's medical records from multiple providers. "Now, consumers will have medical information from various institutions organized into one view covering allergies, conditions, immunizations, lab results, medications, procedures and vitals, and will receive notifications when their data is updated," Apple said in a news release.[67] The list of providers agreeing to share information has been growing steadily since then and includes private practices and world-class medical centers. Users can share with a doctor or family member these records and other health data collected by the iPhone from an Apple watch or a fitness tracker.

---

67   Apple, "Apple announces effortless solution bringing health records to iPhone," news release, January 24, 2018, https://www.apple.com/newsroom/2018/01/apple-announces-effortless-solution-bringing-health-records-to-iPhone/.

Regulatory Approval

My office receives cold calls every week from companies that have developed new software or platforms for virtual care. They all promise to interact seamlessly, but when we have them demonstrate how the product works, issues usually arise. Another problem is that many of these technologies need government approval, such as from the US Food and Drug Administration or in our case, Health Canada. Many of the companies say they are going through the process, and it is taking longer than they could have imagined. In other words, they are walking across the bridge as they build it. Eventually the big technology companies will power themselves into the virtual care space and the regulators will accede to what's happening.

In the meantime, we can expect to see a lot of speed bumps and some spectacular crashes on the road to virtual care. Startups will produce diagnostics that fail to live up to their claims, hopefully not involving the kind of criminal fraud that the Silicon Valley blood-testing company Theranos perpetuated. Prominent investors and drugstore chains wasted millions of dollars on Theranos based on false claims that it had come up with a machine that could diagnose many illnesses from a pinprick of blood. Other companies are being cautious. Thriva, a London-based company offering blood tests by subscription to consumers, was careful to make clear that it was not directly offering diagnoses: "Take health into your own hands," its website urged consumers, quickly followed by noting that results would have to be sent to an approved lab and analyzed by doctors.

Big tech companies exercise similar caution by portraying their monitoring devices as encouraging healthy habits, not diagnosing illnesses. At this writing, the Samsung website shows a woman wearing a Galaxy smartwatch in bed to monitor blood oxygen during sleep.

That's obviously not something healthy people need to do, but the fine print warns: "Intended for general wellness and fitness purposes only. Not intended for use in detection, diagnosis, treatment of any medical condition or disease."[68] Down the road, however, virtual care will be relying more and more on such devices for medically supervised detection, diagnosis, and treatment. The manufacturers are accumulating data for research and development of wearable diagnostic devices and staking out their turf in the field in anticipation of future regulatory approval.

EXPERIMENTATION AND PERSISTENCE

Trying new things and persisting to find success is how we make progress in medicine. My specialty, transplant surgery, is a good example. When Dr. Thomas Starzl pioneered liver transplant surgery in the 1960s, his first several patients died during or not long after the operations. It may have seemed to outsiders that he was killing his patients, but they would have died without the transplant, too, because they had end-stage liver failure. Dr. Starzl paused his efforts and did more research but did not give up trying liver transplants. A few years passed before one of his patients survived a year. Dr. Starzl is remembered as a much-honored, world-renowned scientist, deservedly because of his persistence.

---

68   Samsung, "Measuring your body composition with the Galaxy Watch4 series," samsung.com, August 16, 2021.

The Care Gap

Two factors that can create a gap in virtual care involve availability of providers and use of technology. People turning to virtual care should be able to access the right kind of provider. If, for example, not enough physicians or specialists are participating and available, how does the system deal with that situation? This brings us back to our previous discussion of allied healthcare professionals practicing at the top of their license. In most places, nurse practitioners or advanced-practice nurses (career titles vary by jurisdiction) can prescribe, diagnose, and treat patients, in some jurisdictions without physician oversight. The oversight requirements have been a contentious issue for many years, but I believe they will be diminished or done away with for the reasons discussed in the previous four chapters. Technology for the remote, real-time monitoring of patients will become more widely available and easier to use.

If we are not there yet, some might ask, why am I predicting this future with such confidence? I personally have seen plenty of conditions that used to require treatment for two weeks in the hospital and now no longer require hospital admission. Even when COVID-19 was filling up ICUs, we were able to stand up a program to manage less sick but already hospitalized COVID patients at home by applying the right concepts, equipment, and human resources. Being able to do things you wouldn't have conceived of a year or a few years ago is just the nature of modern medicine and the pace of technological development.

Where a care gap cannot be overcome, virtual care must have an in-person fallback, which some refer to as a hybrid system. For example, medical rehab and geriatrics are two areas in which we have found virtual care at home to be welcomed and successful for some patients but inappropriate for others. A lot of elderly people are uncomfortable with technology, live alone, and do not have close family members or friends who would be able to help them participate. The healthcare system also must treat people in various unstable living situations, including homelessness, and the common and easiest response is to admit them to a hospital. If we believe hospital-at-home treatment would be better for their well-being, a more equitable solution must be developed. A health system should consider developing some community-based care centers for those patients, which would save public money compared with a hospital stay.

THE GENERATION GAP

Interest in virtual care increased markedly in 2020 among all age groups because of the pandemic, but Advisory Board consultants found that 18- to 54-year-olds were four times more likely to consider switching doctors if their providers do not offer a digital experience compared with people ages 55 and up.[69] In a series of surveys called the COVID-19 Tracker, the Harris Poll found that about two-thirds of US adults who tried telehealth would continue using it after the pandemic. Somewhat fewer people were willing in suburban and rural areas than in urban areas, but the striking finding was that 48 percent of seniors would continue using telehealth—not a majority, but not a huge fall-off by age. The Harris Poll also asked, "If you were able to conduct much of your regular medical appointments via telehealth or virtual services, would you ever consider getting rid of your primary care doctor?" Half of the

---

69 Lindsay Conway, Kaci Brooks, Jinia Sarkar, and Sophie Tan, "The Virtual Patient Experience Today," Advisory Board, January 31, 2022, https://www.advisory.com/topics/market-trends/2022/01/the-virtual-patient-experience-today.

millennials and younger generations said yes, but only 8 percent of the seniors said yes.[70]

The criteria that determine whether virtual care is appropriate for someone apply to people's individual circumstances and their current condition. We have used the hospital-at-home program for patients who recently had surgery, heart failure, and acute exacerbation of chronic obstructive lung disease, emphysema, cellulitis, and urinary tract infections. A patient can be a great candidate for the hospital-at-home program for their congestive heart failure but if they get sick with something else and need an intravenous medication, they must be admitted to the hospital. We are not going to send someone home from the hospital to have a family member administer a morphine drip for an acute symptom. But where feasible, healthcare needs to take a lesson from other industries that give customers a choice of doing business face-to-face or online, as is common in banking and retail.

It Comes Down to Control

Satisfaction with virtual care often comes down to people feeling they have more control over their treatment. Healthcare administrators and policymakers have quantitative data verifying the programs' effectiveness. For example, I see data showing my hospital-at-home program's very low rates of returns to the emergency room and readmissions. Patients evaluate their experience before, during, and after a visit, whether it is virtual or in person. They see how easy it is to

---

70　"The Great Awakening," Harris Poll, March 15, 2021, https://theharrispoll.com/briefs/the-great-awakening/.

make an appointment, how long they must wait, whether they feel they are getting quality care, and whether their issues are resolved. A virtual visit may offer convenience (not having to drive somewhere and find and pay for parking) and feel safer (not being in a waiting room full of sick people), benefits that add to a feeling of being in control of the experience. Being able to schedule or reschedule appointments and choose providers, such as pharmacies or lab sites online, adds to the feeling of control. Now

> **Satisfaction with virtual care often comes down to people feeling they have more control over their treatment.**

imagine that while they are waiting, the virtual system's AI offers the patient videos customized to their health issues and follows up afterward with personalized answers on their care, prescriptions, and referrals.

Circling Back

Entrepreneurs ranging from startups to multinationals have seen rich opportunities in virtual care for more than 15 years. The necessity of expanding virtual care during the pandemic led to innovations in telehealth and hospital-at-home programs. Increased and enduring acceptance of virtual care has been seen across society, although some physicians are reluctant to embrace such a big change in their practice. Some technology innovations that could help power virtual care have failed to work as promoted, and others are being marketed as wellness or fitness aids to get around regulatory approval barriers. Those barriers are likely to fall, and the efficiency and convenience of virtual care is likely to grow over time as technology develops. Gaps will always remain that necessitate a hybrid system in which face-to-face care is available where needed.

Virtual care done right can provide people a more personalized service in which they have more control over scheduling and choice of providers. In the process, people's medical records and sensitive personal data must be online in databases that can be accessed by authorized staff more widely than what has been standard in the medical establishment. The next chapter explores the implications of online data sharing and what can be done to balance expectations of privacy with people's autonomy to choose their providers and seek care anywhere or everywhere.

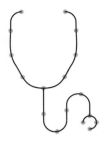

CHAPTER 11

The Issue of Privacy
and Autonomy

Seeing more people wearing smart watches capable of monitoring vital signs gave me an idea, and in 2022 I had the opportunity to bounce that idea off some people who know a lot more than me about technology, Apple engineers in Cupertino, California. Their company was marketing the Apple Watch as having health benefits because available apps could notify users about irregular heart rhythms and display heart-rate measurements, oxygen saturation, and other fitness metrics. Since the user could see that data on the iPhone Health app, I asked whether the smart watch also could easily transmit it to a handheld device that could be issued to doctors or other health professionals. I was envisioning a dashboard display of vital signs that would be useful in clinical settings, perhaps displayed on augmented reality eyeglasses worn by the healthcare provider. The engineers said they had not really thought about developing such an app because its existence would raise privacy issues. I respect Apple for spending a lot of time, energy, and money on privacy, but I hope we can work out convenient and systematic ways for ordinary people to authorize transmission of data from wearable technology to their healthcare providers. Making it happen with minimal friction and maximum security is a challenge, but one worth addressing.

A few months after I talked with the engineers, Apple put out a 60-page report outlining its vision of using technology to empower people to be intelligent guardians of their own health.[71] The report gave me confidence that we are well on our way toward that goal. The first part of the progress involves the tens of thousands of apps that let users see their own everyday health data. Apple said its Health app alone could store over 150 different types of health data from Apple Watch, iPhone, and connected third-party apps and devices. Second, medical research is being advanced through studies in which users agree to share their data. And finally, the report began to address my interest in streamlining secure communications between people and their healthcare providers:

> "In addition to having conversations in person around data from the Health app, patients can also easily export a PDF of their ECG [electrocardiogram] app results on Apple Watch to share with their doctor. And at participating institutions in the US, patients can use the Health Sharing feature in the Health app to share categories of Health app data with their physician. When patients choose to share this data, their healthcare team can view the shared data in a web-based view in their own EHR [electronic health record] system and review trends and

---

71   Apple, "Empowering people to live a healthier day," apple.com, July 2022, https://www.apple.com/newsroom/pdfs/Health-Report-September-2022.pdf.

changes over time. This feature builds on Health Records on iPhone, which creates a direct, encrypted connection between participating health institutions and a patient's iPhone so patients can see a central view of their allergies, conditions, immunizations, lab results, medications, procedures, and vitals directly within the Health app."[72]

Many patients lack the resources to own and use such sophisticated technology, and it won't spread through our institutions uniformly, but everyone will benefit in the long run from these initiatives by Apple and many other companies. It's like the way that aerospace research led to everyday products, such as scratch-resistant eyeglasses. Scientists will make discoveries from the data, technologists will develop better ways to protect its privacy, and people will talk more with their loved ones about how easy it can be to measure their wellness.

Who Owns Our Medical Data?

The Apple engineers who raised the privacy issue were starting from an assumption that the data belongs to the individual, as it should. Who else would it belong to? The answer can vary more than people realize. Many US states have laws saying medical records belong to the provider, practice, or facility that created the record, while US federal law gives patients the rights to inspect, review, or receive a copy of those records. In simple terms, one might say providers own the records and patients own the information in those records. Of course, it's not that simple when electronic records can be stored and shared en masse. Digital technology allows data to be easily searched, sold, and stolen, as we discussed in chapter 6.

---

72   Ibid.

Laws governing control of medical records are made or proposed based not only on the interests of people's health but also the latest concerns about national security and crime or proponents' financial and moral motivations. Amid concerns about terrorism after the September 11 attacks in 2001, US law enforcement gained a greater ability to secretly access all kinds of data, including medical records. Presumably the authorities would need to sweep up health records quickly in response to a disease outbreak to determine whether it involved bioterrorism or a public-health emergency. Hacking of medical records and ransomware attacks on hospitals led to calls for government intervention to tighten control of records. Business interests, not criminal intent, come into play when hospitals can benefit financially from selling the vast amount of personal medical information they collect. Pharmaceutical companies have been buying warehouses full of data to develop products that can be quite profitable, and they have not had to compensate the people whose information was exploited. Monetizing consumer data with as little government regulation as possible also is an essential business model for the big technology companies hoping to profit from making virtual care more convenient through digital innovation. People's right to privacy overlaps with some of society's most hotly contested social issues, such as abortion, which we will discuss later in this chapter.

Where I live, personal medical information increasingly belongs to the provincial government. "The Québec Health Record (QHR) is a secure provincial tool that collects and stores certain health information about everyone who receives care in Québec. It is an automated and mandatory process that does not require any professional to do anything," a government website explains.[73] In a public health system, the government says it needs full visibility into where its spending is going and how resources should be allocated. Other stated reasons for a government-controlled system making medical records accessible to any authorized healthcare provider are to expedite care anywhere, especially in an emergency, avoid wasteful duplication of tests and examinations, and prevent adverse drug interactions. Those goals are commendable, but I believe the person whose information is being generated should remain in control of it. We already have discussed a workaround called synthetic data that would give public health authorities and researchers valid information and insights without violating anyone's privacy.

BUSINESS TOOLS SWEEP UP PERSONAL DATA

Major privacy breaches can happen inadvertently, as we learned in June 2022 when *The Markup*, a New York-based nonprofit news organization covering technology, revealed this: "A tracking tool installed on many hospitals' websites has been collecting patients' sensitive health information—including details about their medical conditions, prescriptions, and doctor's appointments—and sending it to Facebook." The investigators found the tracker called Meta Pixel on 33 of the websites of 100 top US hospitals.[74] People

---

73   Quebec, "The Quebec Health Record," quebec.ca, accessed December 15, 2022, https://www.quebec.ca/en/health/your-health-information/quebec-health-record/about.

74   Todd Feathers, Simon Fondrie-Teitler, Angie Waller, and Surya Mattu, "Facebook Is Receiving Sensitive Medical Information from Hospital Websites," The Markup, June 16, 2022, https://themarkup.org/pixel-hunt/2022/06/16/facebook-is-receiving-sensitive-medical-information-from-hospital-websites.

were using the websites for convenient features, such as scheduling appointments online. The hospital administrators surely never realized that popular software their technicians installed from Meta, the parent company of Facebook, would send details, such as the name of the doctor and the reason for the appointment, to Facebook. We don't know what, if anything, Facebook did with those data transfers, which were a betrayal of the hospitals' legal obligation to protect confidential health information. Meta says it has filtering systems that can detect and remove any potentially sensitive health data swept up by its business tools, but privacy advocates remain skeptical.

The Need for Personal Autonomy

We have experienced two sustained uproars that reflect how difficult it is for society to agree on medical privacy and autonomy issues. The first involved widespread hesitancy to take the COVID-19 vaccines. The government has every right to declare a public health emergency and require appropriate protections. People have control over their own bodies, so they have the right to make an individual decision not to get vaccinated. Those two conflicting rights left a lot of ground for disagreement over requirements on when and where people had to prove they were vaccinated to enter workplaces or public venues. Another ongoing public battle resulted from the US Supreme Court's decision in June 2022 to overturn *Roe v. Wade*. In that case, abortion-rights advocates have argued that people should have control over their own bodies and have the right to make an individual decision to end a pregnancy. Ironically, some of these same people were shaming those refusing to get vaccinated and asking for government mandates.

People legitimately fear that once we give governments access to private medical information, it will be used not just for public health but for other purposes, such as to police or control people and their behavior, or for some nefarious purpose. Those fears underlay conspiracy theories about vaccines. In my healthcare system in Montreal, when we set up mass vaccination centers and mass testing centers for COVID, statistically, the people

> People legitimately fear that once we give governments access to private medical information, it will be used not just for public health but for other purposes.

who didn't show up tended to be from certain ethnic and cultural religious minorities, immigrants who were distrustful of government. We had to go seek them out and add an extra layer of comfort by setting up testing and vaccination centers in their community gathering places. In my province, the government set up a portal to begin to give people direct access to their personal medical history. But this website and other similar ones elsewhere require patients to prove their identity by submitting confidential information, such as a social security number or income tax data that they may have to search for on other websites. The intention is to protect privacy, but we need to do so in a way people don't find tedious, inefficient, or suspicious.

Privacy and autonomy are like opposite sides of a coin in that you can't have one without the other. As healthcare becomes increasingly decentralized, as we have more choices about where we seek care virtually or in person, counting on providers or the government to maintain and distribute our information is not the route to preserving our privacy. People must learn to take personal control of the information as an autonomous agent. Having control over one's own healthcare information is basically having control over one's body and one's destiny.

This autonomy doesn't have to be burdensome if institutions provide secure, interconnected, and user-friendly platforms. Consider how we control the money in our personal bank accounts. Nobody would want to give control of their account to the government or the bank or be forced to visit their specific bank branch to find out how much money is in the account. Digital tools online and at ATMs make it easy to get that information and control the money from practically anywhere in a secure, interconnected system. Technology companies similarly give us platforms on which we can control our digital personas from anywhere. We have autonomy over what we choose to display on Facebook, LinkedIn, or Twitter, although the corporate owners of those sites and the government make rules and set limits.

> **Having control over one's own healthcare information is basically having control over one's body and one's destiny.**

Policymakers should insist that as people take more control over their personal medical information, they demonstrate that they have put appropriate protections in place. This kind of precaution is familiar to anyone who has been instructed by a website to use a stronger password or two-factor authentication or who has been ordered by an employer to use a virtual private network (VPN) to work from home. The healthcare industry is far behind in providing platforms that people trust and are enthusiastic about using. I can envision people I know getting a thrill posting on social media or being excited to find their bank's ATM when they need cash while traveling. I don't know people who are thrilled to use any healthcare provider apps.

The Rough Road to Privacy

The expectation of personal privacy has been a tough issue in healthcare for a long time. For many centuries, private rooms were an exception in hospitals, which tended to have wards in which patients' beds were separated at most with a curtain. This design saved money on construction and made it easier for staff to monitor their charges without today's technology. Concerns about infection control contributed to the move toward private rooms. In a 2015 reconstruction of my hospital, we eliminated three- or four-bed rooms and redesigned the emergency room to give patients their own physical space because we thought that privacy was important. Being able to overhear what is happening nearby remains common in many emergency rooms, clinics, and doctors' offices around the world.

Those of us who work in hospitals all have stories we can tell, sometimes on ourselves, about being overheard talking about patients at the wrong time, in the wrong place, or in front of the wrong people. Medical or surgical residents chat in crowded elevators about unfortunate complications they just saw in the operating room—for example, a blood vessel was cut by mistake. That's inappropriate conversation for a public setting, and in the worst-case scenario the patient's family members happen to be in the elevator and realize whose surgery they are discussing. These days, physicians share photographs taken with their smartphones of conditions they are evaluating, such as patients' wounds or lesions. Consulting with colleagues is expected, but sharing photographs of patients in an unsecured messaging app is an impermissible infringement on patient privacy.

Privacy laws already create a lot of tensions in hospitals because relatives are not entitled to information that the patient has not provided written consent to share. It is quite common for relatives to badger healthcare administrators, doctors, nurses, and the patients themselves over these restrictions and insist they are entitled to know exactly who is doing what to their loved ones and why it is being done. Laws have established that the patient has certain control over personal medical information. We all must exercise that control in ways that make sense for us and our families, and it is up to the healthcare system to keep privacy measures updated. The design of facilities with more walls separating patient spaces has been a good step, and we also need to design firewalls in our digital systems as they become more interconnected and widely accessible.

Blockchain Can Help Secure Data

Blockchain technology may be the key to securing private patient information. As we discussed in chapter 3, Estonia leaped ahead of other countries in adopting that technology, which secures data by distributing it across a network in blocks that are chained together via cryptography. The Estonian government set up an e-Health task force in 2014 that involved the gamut of healthcare stakeholders in its strategic planning.[75] They set goals of collecting high-quality health data from people and always using it in transparent and controlled ways. The intention was to give people control of their personalized data so they could actively participate in managing their own health, but also so they could opt in to sharing it for research and development or in any of the ways we have discussed that people should be getting healthcare. By 2016, the northern European country began

---

75   Government of the Republic of Estonia, "Estonian Health Strategic Development Plan 2020," November 27, 2015, https://apo.org.au/node/252426.

using blockchain to record every access or change to patients' medical records. Both the patient and any medical professional would always see the latest version. That system remains an outlier today, but an example of what we should be aspiring to in terms of giving individuals full control over their own personal medical histories. A detailed report on the challenges and issues involved is available from the European Union Blockchain Observatory & Forum.[76]

Many people associate blockchain with its use in the cryptocurrency markets, but that sector's issues are not relevant to its application for healthcare data. For individuals, using a blockchain key to access their data would be no more complicated than using a PIN code to access an ATM or a password to access a website. The security advantages of blockchain are that information storage is not centralized in institutions but is distributed, and every access to the information is recorded in a digital ledger. Once a block of data is created and time-stamped, any tampering would be visible across the network. Our current system has been vulnerable to ransomware attacks in which hackers lock all the patient files. Some hospitals have ended up paying ransom because they needed to get back to work saving people's lives. No system will ever offer a perfect defense against hackers, but individual, encrypted data stored in a decentralized system makes for a less inviting target. Cyber defense must be part of any strategy for the digital transfer and storage of healthcare information.

Medical data is precious. Researchers need the trust of diverse people and institutions to make sure the data they are working with is representative, so the treatments they develop will work across populations. Increasing recognition during the pandemic of the issue of

---

76   European Commission, "Blockchain Applications in the Healthcare
      Sector," February 9, 2022, https://digital-strategy.ec.europa.eu/en/library/
      blockchain-applications-healthcare-sector.

equity in healthcare delivery has reinforced our sensitivity to respecting how personal autonomy and privacy concerns must be respected as we go into people's neighborhoods, build relationships, and deal with them on their level. Lessons from the pandemic, in which we had to persuade fearful people to take vaccines should carry through to promoting everyday wellness. We know enough about the social determinants of health to know that where and how one lives is a very important factor in medical issues.

Circling Back

Privacy is an issue healthcare has been addressing for centuries, instilling ethical standards for providers to protect confidentiality and, within our lifetimes, redesigning facilities to put walls, not curtains, between beds. Now with decentralization of care and the democratization of knowledge and technology, we are in a new era of digital privacy concerns we must urgently address to avoid unintended consequences. Our technology companies must provide convenient, accessible tools to give people autonomy and control over their personal medical data. Individuals must take control with their eyes open to the personal responsibility and accountability involved. Our policymakers, providers, and professional schools share in the responsibility of healthcare being successfully centered on the people who use it. The next chapter explores what all the stakeholders in our healthcare systems should be doing to get the best outcomes from the changes we see happening.

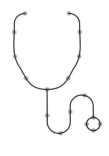

CHAPTER 12

What Now?

Canada's 13 provincial and territorial premiers differ widely on many issues but were unified on one demand when they met in person in July 2022 for the first time in three years. They wanted more money from the federal government for healthcare. I'll spare you the details of the quibbling over budgetary math and funding formulas. I'm telling this story because it perfectly represents the way talking about money dominates our high-level decision-making about healthcare. Public accounts of the meeting focused on what the federal percentage share of healthcare funding is or should be. Left to be discussed some other time and place, maybe someday, were the important questions: How should that money be spent? What outcomes should be expected?

In my dream version of that meeting in picturesque Victoria, British Columbia, federal health ministry officials show up with strategic plans aimed at expanding and updating services, eliminating variations in care, and trimming costs. Of course, the premiers insist that each province or territory has unique circumstances, and each should control its healthcare spending with no strings attached to the federal money. That's their opening position, but they come prepared to compromise on specific accountability measures that the evidence showed were necessary. Experts in the intricacies of healthcare funding have worked out most of the compromises in advance after public hearings in which people were able to tell the policymakers what they wanted out of their healthcare system. By the time the premiers get to Victoria, they have signed off on some big policy changes. Recalling how COVID-19 put stress on their hospitals and other providers, they drop their insistence that providers be licensed at the provincial level, which makes it hard for doctors and nurses to work in another jurisdiction, even temporarily or virtually. The premiers recognize that technology is transforming healthcare delivery, and they make sure their spending plans are flexible enough to shift money from outdated categories to the latest developments.

Okay, back to reality: users of a healthcare system and its other stakeholders become defensive about any proposals to change it. We have seen that defensiveness in the United States with resistance to plans such as Obamacare that aimed to broaden access to health insurance. The Canada Health Act, federal legislation that established publicly funded health insurance, has such devout support that politicians fear being considered "unCanadian" if they bring up needed changes. But we must be undeterred in discussing what we should be doing differently.

> **Users of a healthcare system and its other stakeholders become defensive about any proposals to change it.**

The Role of Professional Schools

Healthcare policymakers and providers cannot accomplish necessary changes without involving the professional schools. Traditional curricula must change, or else the graduates of the professional schools will emerge unprepared to function in the rapidly changing environment. They must learn how to provide virtual care and become comfortable with extended-reality technology. When I went to medical school, we learned anatomy dissecting donated cadavers. Does learning anatomy on cadavers, as I did, make sense in a world in which experiencing virtual reality in the metaverse is literally child's play? Our medical-school students can see that we are lagging other industries in digital technology. One excellent medical school is offering a work-around: select medical students can pursue a separate master's degree in medical innovation, learning things they need to know but that the traditional curriculum doesn't find time to cover. Even if an individual college wants to change its curriculum, it must do so cautiously because curricula generally must meet national standards for accreditation.

The need for more primary-care providers, which has reached crisis levels in some places, has led policymakers to reevaluate who does what in healthcare delivery. If we are going to have advanced-practice nurses or physician assistants, not doctors, as primary care providers, the professional schools must adapt to that reality. I am affiliated with one of the world's premier medical schools, and as I write this, even we have not adequately addressed these issues. As virtual care expands, we must decide who is qualified to perform different roles, including running programs such as hospital at home. I think the doctors in charge can be general practitioners, not specialists, and that we should be training nurses to perform much of the work in these programs. These points may provoke resistance or anxiety among my medical colleagues for various reasons. They fear medical malpractice issues, are uncomfortable with new technology, or worry about not being sufficiently reimbursed by insurers or compensated for care in which they don't have hands on a patient in their office. Updating the curricula in professional schools is more likely to change attitudes among newcomers to the profession than among those already settled in.

Updating Skills and Job Descriptions

Most professional licensing bodies require a certain amount of continuing education, but it is usually very granular. Doctors or nurses might take a one-day course on a new medication, method, or treatment. No matter how useful this education might be, it won't change anyone's views of how they should be practicing medicine in a world changing so fast that entire job descriptions must be scrapped or reinvented. As we noted in chapter 7, AI is rapidly developing the ability to perform certain pattern-recognition diagnoses currently done by highly paid specialists in radiology and dermatology. If I were working in those specialties, or in pathology, I would be worried about my job and would be seeking fresh training. I might need to learn about validating algorithms or how to configure, manage, and assess the latest machines.

> Clearly, we should not be paying large sums to train specialists to perform jobs that could be done as well or better by AI.

Healthcare policymakers must pay attention to these technology trends because they affect the number of positions that should be set aside in medical schools and residencies. Where the public is funding the training, budget decisions made by politicians can reverberate for years. I have seen this happen in Canada, where an ill-considered decision in the 1990s that we were training too many doctors resulted in a years-long doctor shortage. Comparisons across developed nations show wide variations in the ratios of doctors and hospital beds to population and in spending on healthcare. The United States and Canada infamously spend more on healthcare per capita than many European countries but don't get better outcomes. Explaining the disparity is far beyond the scope of this book, so let's focus on the interplay between wasteful spending and decisions about who should be doing what. Clearly, we should not be paying large sums to train specialists to perform jobs that could be done as well or better by AI.

Deciding Who Does What and Where

Employers play an increasing role in deciding how to deploy doctors, at least in the United States. About three-fourths of US doctors are employees of hospital systems or corporations.[77] The share of US doctors in private practice is shrinking fast and seems likely to continue to do so because many are getting close to retirement age. In contrast, most Canadian doctors are free agents, with public funding of universal health insurance. One of my colleagues at a leading US medical center told me at a conference about how it was able to set up a large-scale hospital-at-home program. It had the same advantages as the smaller program I started, including lowering costs and protecting against running out of hospital beds, but the US hospital could assign doctors to the program because they were employees. The institution could take a loss on insurance reimbursement for the time being to

---

77   Avalare Health, COVID-19's Impact on Acquisitions of Physician Practices and Physician Employment 2019–2021 (Physicians Advocacy Institute, 2022), http://www.physiciansadvocacyinstitute.org/Portals/0/assets/docs/PAI-Research/PAI%20Avalere%20Physician%20Employment%20Trends%20Study%202019-21%20Final.pdf.

realize long-term cost savings. Rollout of similar programs in Canada has been more limited because free-agent doctors are insulated from the institutional costs and focused on how participating might immediately affect their compensation.

Canada's combination of a single-payer system with private providers is unusual. The UK, Australia, and many other countries with universal healthcare combine the single-payer concept with predominately public healthcare delivery. Other countries, such as Germany, have a combination of public and private insurance paying for universal healthcare. Hybrid public-private systems are better ways to pay for and deliver healthcare. When I see the constant squabbling by Canada's physician unions over how to divide the public money, I think something needs to give to accommodate the significant changes already happening in healthcare.

Our current healthcare systems in North America give users a lot of leeway to decide where they should be treated, and often they inappropriately choose the emergency room. We must manage and change their expectations, a task for which private health-insurance companies have shown more aptitude than government officials have. The healthcare network I direct has learned to engage in community outreach to overcome language and cultural barriers with our large immigrant population in Montreal. Few areas have so much diversity, but none of us in healthcare administration should think we are in ivory towers and that people will come to us for timely care. They often come to our hospitals when it is far too late if we fail to establish a relationship with them when they are still healthy.

THE ROAD MAP TO CARE EVERYWHERE

- **The users of a healthcare system** should be advocating for their own interests, which means they get timely, quality care in convenient locations without overpaying. They need to understand those convenient locations may be a shopping center or their living room.
- **Policymakers** should understand their deliverable is timely access to the right high-quality care at the right time and in the right place by the right person with the right outcomes. Where we don't offer that care, they must figure out how to fix the system.
- **Professionals** who work in that system should figure out what training, resources, and support they need to provide that high-quality care.
- **The professional schools** should understand what will in the future be expected of the people they train. They should be questioning whether they are training the right people in the right way.

The Role of Self-Care

A lot of people were brought up to be passive participants in their healthcare. They're not used to demanding access to their own personal medical information or control of that data. They tend to accept whatever they're told about what treatment they should be getting by whom and where. In my prior work as a surgeon, only a few patients over the span of 20 years asked me what I thought were the most important questions: "Have you done this procedure before?

What were your results?" Maybe they were just happy to have gotten in the door, or maybe they assumed they were expected to be passive participants. After all, they were labeled as patients, not consumers.

Being active in our healthcare means taking more responsibility for ourselves and what we can do to stay well and prevent disease. The best time to get that attitude ingrained in people is childhood. Our elementary school curricula should include lessons about nutrition and exercise that really take hold, get children thinking, and make lifelong impressions—the way boot camp does for military recruits. Wellness programs in our society tend to be reactive—taking aim at targets such as smoking or sugary drinks. We have had some successes with those one-off interventions. People quit smoking, used sun protection to prevent skin cancer, and joined weight-loss programs. We also have saved lives and suffering with upstream medical interventions, such as using colonoscopy and mammography screenings to reduce advanced colon and breast cancers. But we need more coherent and systematic programs to intervene earlier in people's lives. Wellness interventions should be built into prenatal and postnatal care. The training of doctors and nurses should reflect how much of a priority it is to prevent chronic disease. We can enlist sports and entertainment celebrities to reinforce the message. Once someone is 60, morbidly obese, not exercising, and smoking, it's usually too late to intervene successfully.

Obesity is an epidemic in North America, leading to unsustainable burdens on the healthcare system to treat heart disease, high blood pressure, cardiovascular disease, and diabetes. It is getting worse, not better. Even while we make progress in some treatment areas, such as cancer care, chronic, preventable diseases are taxing our medical system as we also face growing incidences of mental health issues and

Alzheimer's disease. The need to control ever-rising healthcare costs should be a major priority for society.

The traditional, paternalistic tendencies of doctor-patient relationships have left healthcare behind other industries in giving people tools and information to look after their own interests. Paul Keckley, a US healthcare analyst based in Nashville, contends that promoting more self-care would help alleviate staff shortages. "The health system is staffed to the presumption that most consumers are incapable of acting rationally about their healthcare and its associated costs," Keckley wrote.[78] Large corporations such as Amazon and CVS that have set their sights on disrupting healthcare will take a more consumer-oriented approach, relying on people's increasing acceptance of technology to perform tasks at home on themselves that were once done by clinical providers.

Circling back

Throughout this book, we have alluded to the need for everyone to take on more responsibility for the healthcare of themselves and their loved ones. We also have discussed the importance of the social determinants of health, which individuals, policymakers, and providers must work together to prioritize addressing. To end up in a better place, we must train our healthcare professionals to function in a rapidly changing environment. Professional schools must meet future needs as technology redefines jobs and makes it possible to deliver quality care in less centralized settings. In that much better place, individuals will have more control over their bodies, more say in their

---

78   Paul Keckley, "Solving Healthcare Workforce Shortages Requires Taking Self-Care More Seriously," August 8, 2022, https://www.paulkeckley.com/the-keckley-report/2022/8/8/ solving-healthcare-workforce-shortages-requires-taking-self-care-more-seriously.

care, and will be better informed about how to manage their lives to avoid chronic, preventable diseases. Together, we will have a more sustainable healthcare system.

Conclusion

The 1960s American television science-fiction show *Star Trek* had a catchphrase so memorable that it lives on as an internet meme. The starship's Captain Kirk would call upon his medical officer, Leonard McCoy, to go above and beyond his normal duties. At that point, McCoy would say, "I'm a doctor, not an engineer," or "I'm a surgeon, not a psychiatrist." Well, here I am a surgeon, not a health-care economist, telling you how we need to reengineer our systems because circumstances are changing at what sci-fi calls warp speed.

I can't write a prescription for a perfect system to finance and deliver healthcare for two monumental reasons. One is the complexity of systems and networks. As explained in chapter 2, healthcare is a "complex adaptive system" whose many components have complex rules, and it is a constantly changing system in which individuals interact in unpredictable and paradoxical ways. The second big reason I can't prescribe a perfect system is that healthcare innovation is constrained by entrenched interests that vary by jurisdiction. The example I gave in the last chapter was Canada's single-payer system, in which federal and provincial politicians must agree on how to control the spending, while doctors are free agents represented in budget negotiations by unions. But wherever you are in the world, I am sure you have shaken your head in amazement, confusion, or disgust over how some medical cost was calculated. I have spent most of my life working in hospitals and couldn't tell you the real cost of any given procedure because we don't operate in a simple free market—far from it.

I believe hybrid public and private systems can do the best job financing and delivering healthcare. For comparison, around the world, private schools exist as an alternative or a supplement to public schools and receive varying amounts of public money and regulation. As far as I know, no government expects teachers to open their own schools and then pays them based on the numbers of students they enroll and the number of lessons they give. That would be nonsensical, but it seems the equivalent of the Canadian fee-for-service system publicly financing private-practice primary care.

A trend in healthcare economics has been to empower primary care providers and insurers to manage care on the assumptions that people don't know what they need, don't understand what it might cost, and will not spend wisely. Upending those assumptions are the trends of disintermediation, decentralization, and connected care. Digital innovators, ranging from startups to some of the largest pharmaceutical, retail, and technology companies, are offering people new and convenient ways to take more control of their bodies and health.

Technology has made healthcare more of a personal responsibility than it has been since a couple of centuries ago. We can mail off a sample and learn about our DNA. A storefront can offer procedures that used to require equipment and specialists housed only in hospitals. We can strap on a smart watch and monitor our vital signs. Telemedicine and virtual visits are becoming more common, a convenience for anyone whose age, disability, work, or family commitments make getting to a doctor's office a burden on themselves or their caregivers.

The convenience of care everywhere comes with a few catches. The more autonomy people have in where they seek care, the more issues we have sharing their data among providers without jeopardizing privacy. Healthcare is behind other industries in creating interoperable systems so that providers can be interconnected seamlessly for medical data or billing. Trying to pay piecemeal for care everywhere seems chaotic, like instead of getting one check at the end of a restaurant meal you pay each cook, server, and busboy who attended to your needs, and pay for your share of whatever the restaurant spent that week on food, utilities, supplies, and services.

We can order people, or incentivize them, to get all their healthcare in one network for cost savings, but I believe people should have autonomy in deciding where to seek care. That said, I know from experience that health networks offering social services along with medical care save society money by addressing the social determinants of health. Failing to educate people early in life about diet, exercise, and healthy habits leads to chronic diseases downstream that make up the bulk of our collective medical expenses. Encouraging more self-care will be labor-saving for understaffed hospitals while creating jobs in businesses that generate the innovations and devices involved.

I keep coming back to the intractable issue of paying for healthcare because we must address it within the context of the disintermediation we have been discussing. Wherever you are reading this book, you may be familiar with whether you or your government or a private insurer will pay for some medical treatment, unless the rules changed while you weren't watching. The rules must be complex and subject to change because technology is transforming our ability to deliver the right care in the right way in the right place. That goal is a moving target to design a system around.

Because healthcare is becoming more personal, we must make sure people avail themselves of the services that promote wellness, prevent disease, and keep our healthcare delivery systems sustainable. We can't force people to do what they don't want to do, but we need to establish a culture of personal responsibility. We must employ social workers to perform community outreach and education, not just about what services are available, but offer support from prenatal care and birth to death. We must help people prevent disease with good nutrition and exercise and maintain their mental health. Through programs like hospital at home and conversations with patients being treated for life-threatening conditions, we know what people want in their lives: maintaining mental acuity and mobility as much as possible, spending time with loved ones, and independence. The traditional healthcare system we are leaving behind was not built around giving people control. Now that control is within everyone's grasp through a partnership between the providers and the people.

About the Author

Dr. Lawrence Rosenberg is president and CEO of the Integrated Health and Social Services University Network for West-Central Montreal. Before assuming this position in 2015, Dr. Rosenberg was chief of surgical services and then executive director of Montreal's Jewish General Hospital.

Dr. Rosenberg received his MD, CM degree from McGill University, where he completed specialty training in general surgery. He holds an MSc and PhD in experimental surgery from McGill and completed postdoctoral studies and a surgical fellowship in transplantation at the University of Michigan.

Formerly, he was director of the Multi-Organ Transplant Program at Montreal General Hospital, inaugurating McGill University's Pancreas Transplant Program and leading the team that performed the first successful liver transplant at McGill. He was also the past Associate Chair of Surgery (Research) in the McGill Department of Surgery and remains a professor of surgery and medicine at McGill University.

Dr. Rosenberg was named a Chercheur National (national scientist) by the government of Quebec and has served as a consultant on peer-review committees of the Juvenile Diabetes Research Foundation, Diabetes Canada, the Canadian Institutes of Health Research, and the US National Institutes of Health.

Having completed an MEng from the University of Waterloo with concentrations in systems, innovation, and entrepreneurship, Dr. Rosenberg has designed and implemented the first provincial digital health program, including a command center and a hospital-at-home program.

Dr. Rosenberg has extensive experience as a clinician-scientist, educator, and consultant in value-based health systems. He is an acclaimed CEO with a proven track record of success, and leads an award-winning institution that is recognized for its excellence and innovation.